Tackle the GCSE Science essentials with CGP!

OK, so AQA Foundation Level GCSE Combined Science is no walkover.
It can seem overwhelming if you haven't got to grips with the basics,
which is where this brilliant CGP Workbook comes in.

All the questions are at a Grade 1-3 level, so there's nothing too tough to put you off.
Only the most important topics are covered — the ones you need to learn before you
can get any further in GCSE Science. Perfect for helping you get on track.

And since it's a CGP book, there's a bit of fun along the way. If you've read a better
joke about radioactivity in anyone else's Science book, we want to hear about it...

CGP — still the best! ☺

Our sole aim here at CGP is to produce the highest quality books —
carefully written, immaculately presented and dangerously close to being funny.

Then we work our socks off to get them out to you
— at the cheapest possible prices.

Published by CGP

Editors:
Emma Clayton, Laura Collins, Jack Davies, Georgina Fairclough, Katherine Faudemer, Katie Fernandez, Paul Jordin, Sharon Keeley-Holden, Luke Molloy, Sarah Pattison, Hayley Thompson, Sarah Williams.

Contributors:
Philip Armstrong, Barrie Crowther, Janet Cruse-Sawyer, Mark Edwards, Ian Francis and Jamie Sinclair.

With thanks to Emily Forsberg, Charlotte Sheridan and Karen Wells for the proofreading.

With thanks to Jan Greenway for the copyright research.

Data used on page 133 from the Highway Code. © Crown Copyright re-produced under the terms of the Click-Use licence v3.0. http://www.nationalarchives.gov.uk/doc/open-government-licence/version/3/

ISBN: 978 1 78908 407 8

Clipart from Corel®
Printed by Elanders Ltd, Newcastle upon Tyne
Illustrations by: Sandy Gardner Artist, email sandy@sandygardner.co.uk

Based on the classic CGP style created by Richard Parsons.

Text, design, layout and original illustrations © Coordination Group Publications Ltd. (CGP) 2019
All rights reserved.

Photocopying this book is not permitted, even if you have a CLA licence.
Extra copies are available from CGP with next day delivery • 0800 1712 712 • www.cgpbooks.co.uk

Contents

✓ Use the tick boxes to check off the topics you've completed.

How to Use This Book.. 1

Topic B1 — Cell Biology
Cells and Microscopy 2
Cell Differentiation and Specialisation 4
Chromosomes and Mitosis 5
Transport in Cells 6

Topic B2 — Organisation
Cell Organisation in Animals and Plants 8
Enzymes 10
Digestion and Food Tests 12
The Lungs and the Heart 14
Blood and Blood Vessels 16
Health and Disease 18
Transpiration and Translocation 20

Topic B3 — Infection and Response
Pathogens and the Immune System 22
Types of Disease 24
Drugs 26

Topic B4 — Bioenergetics
Photosynthesis 28
Respiration and Exercise 30

Topic B5 — Homeostasis and Response
Homeostasis and the Nervous System 32
Reflexes and Reaction Time 33
Hormones and Controlling Blood Glucose ... 34
Puberty and the Menstrual Cycle 35

Topic B6 — Inheritance, Variation and Evolution
DNA and Chromosomes 36
Reproduction 37
Genetic Diagrams 38
Variation and Evolution 40
Selective Breeding and Genetic Engineering ... 41
Fossils and Classification 42

Topic B7 — Ecology
Competition and Population Size 43
Adaptations 44
Food Chains 45
Using Quadrats and Transects 46
Biodiversity and Human Activity 48

Topic C1 — Atomic Structure and the Periodic Table
Atoms and Elements 50
Compounds and Equations 52
Separating Mixtures 54
Electronic Structure and the Periodic Table ... 56
Metals and Non-Metals 58
Group 1 59
Group 7 60
Group 0 61

Topic C2 — Bonding, Structure and Properties of Matter
Ionic Bonding 62
Covalent Bonding 64
Metallic Bonding 67
States of Matter 68

Topic C3 — Quantitative Chemistry
Relative Formula Mass.....................................70
Conservation of Mass......................................72

Topic C4 — Chemical Changes
Acids and Bases...74
Reactions of Metals..76
Electrolysis...78

Topic C5 — Energy Changes
Exothermic and Endothermic Reactions..........80
Reaction Profiles..82

Topic C6 — The Rate and Extent of Chemical Change
Rates of Reaction..84
Calculating Rates of Reaction..........................86

Topic C7 — Organic Chemistry
Hydrocarbons and Crude Oil............................88
Using Hydrocarbons...90

Topic C8 — Chemical Analysis
Purity and Formulations...................................92

Topic C9 — Chemistry of the Atmosphere
Climate Change and Pollution..........................93

Topic C10 — Using Resources
Finite and Renewable Resources......................94
Potable Water..95

Topic P1 — Energy
Energy Stores and Energy Transfers.................96
Heating and Unwanted Energy Transfers.........98
Power and Efficiency......................................100
Energy Resources and their Uses...................102

Topic P2 — Electricity
Current and Circuits.......................................104
Resistance and I-V Characteristics.................105
Series and Parallel Circuits.............................107
Electricity and Power in the Home.................109
The National Grid...111

Topic P3 — Particle Model of Matter
The Particle Model and Density.....................112
Internal Energy, Changes of State and
    Specific Latent Heat..................................114

Topic P4 — Atomic Structure
The Current Model of the Atom
    and Isotopes..116
Radioactive Decay and Properties of
    Nuclear Radiation......................................118
Half-life..120

Topic P5 — Forces
Forces, Resultant Forces and Work Done......122
Weight, Mass and Gravity..............................124
Forces and Elasticity......................................125
Distance, Speed and Acceleration.................126
Distance- and Velocity-Time Graphs..............128
Newton's Laws...130
Stopping Distances and Reaction Times.......132

Topic P6 — Waves
Waves: The Basics...134
Electromagnetic Waves and Their Uses........136

Topic P7 — Magnetism
Permanent and Induced Magnets..................138

The Periodic Table...140

1

How to Use This Book

- Before trying to use this book, read the following safety information.
- In case of emergency, press the two halves of the book together firmly to close the book.

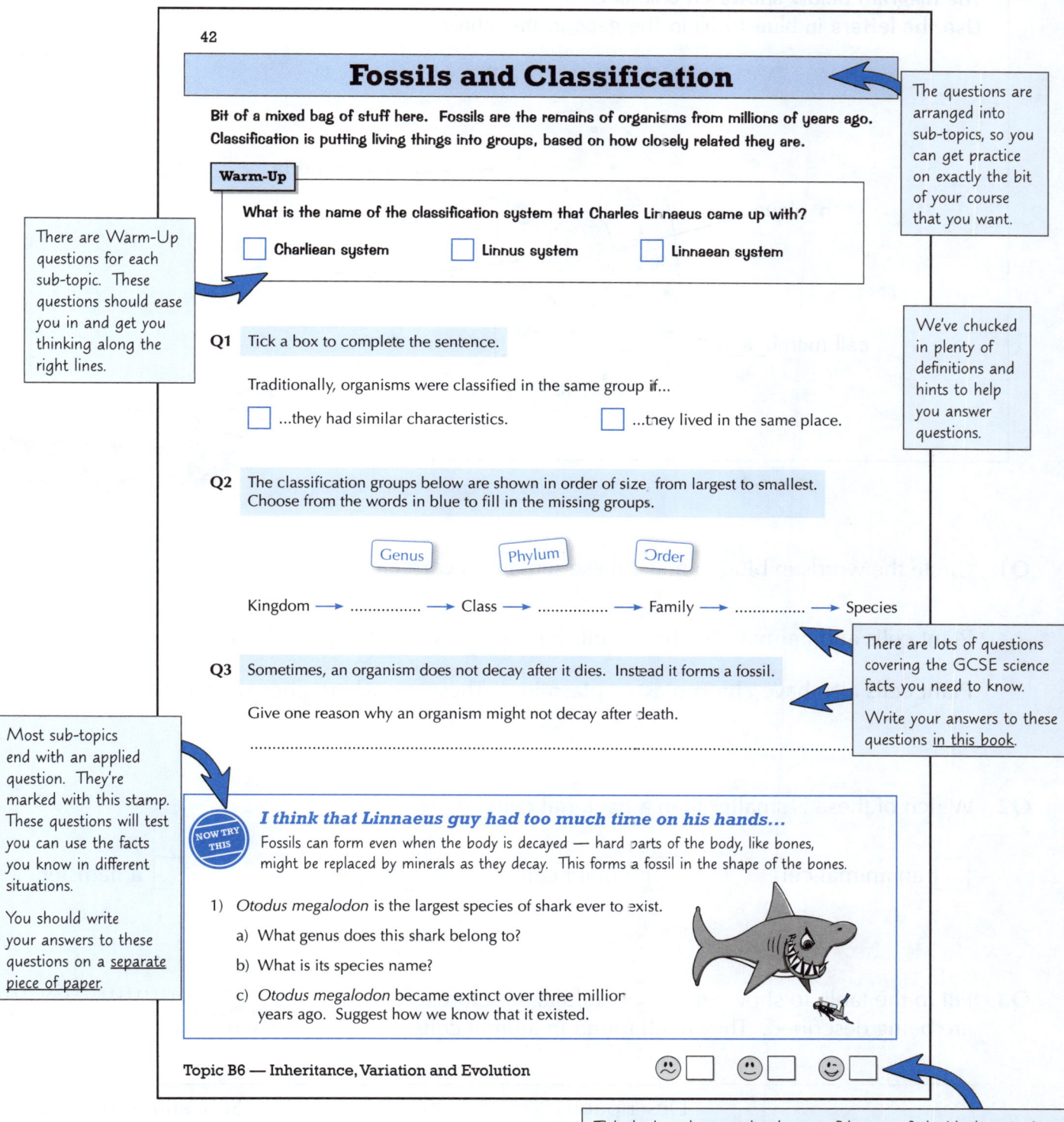

42

Fossils and Classification

Bit of a mixed bag of stuff here. Fossils are the remains of organisms from millions of years ago. Classification is putting living things into groups, based on how closely related they are.

Warm-Up

What is the name of the classification system that Charles Linnaeus came up with?

☐ Charliean system ☐ Linnus system ☐ Linnaean system

The questions are arranged into sub-topics, so you can get practice on exactly the bit of your course that you want.

There are Warm-Up questions for each sub-topic. These questions should ease you in and get you thinking along the right lines.

Q1 Tick a box to complete the sentence.

Traditionally, organisms were classified in the same group if...

☐ ...they had similar characteristics.   ☐ ...they lived in the same place.

Q2 The classification groups below are shown in order of size, from largest to smallest. Choose from the words in blue to fill in the missing groups.

Genus   Phylum   Order

Kingdom → .... → Class → .... → Family → .... → Species

We've chucked in plenty of definitions and hints to help you answer questions.

Q3 Sometimes, an organism does not decay after it dies. Instead it forms a fossil.

Give one reason why an organism might not decay after death.

....

There are lots of questions covering the GCSE science facts you need to know.

Write your answers to these questions in this book.

Most sub-topics end with an applied question. They're marked with this stamp. These questions will test you can use the facts you know in different situations.

You should write your answers to these questions on a separate piece of paper.

> **NOW TRY THIS**
>
> ### I think that Linnaeus guy had too much time on his hands...
>
> Fossils can form even when the body is decayed — hard parts of the body, like bones, might be replaced by minerals as they decay. This forms a fossil in the shape of the bones.
>
> 1) *Otodus megalodon* is the largest species of shark ever to exist.
>   a) What genus does this shark belong to?
>   b) What is its species name?
>   c) *Otodus megalodon* became extinct over three million years ago. Suggest how we know that it existed.

Topic B6 — Inheritance, Variation and Evolution   ☹ ☐ ☺ ☐ 😃 ☐

Tick the box that matches how confident you feel with the questions in each sub-topic. This should help show you which sub-topics you've got a good grasp of, and which you need to work on more.

Topic B1 — Cell Biology

Cells and Microscopy

Welcome to your first page of questions. Don't you just love that new book smell...

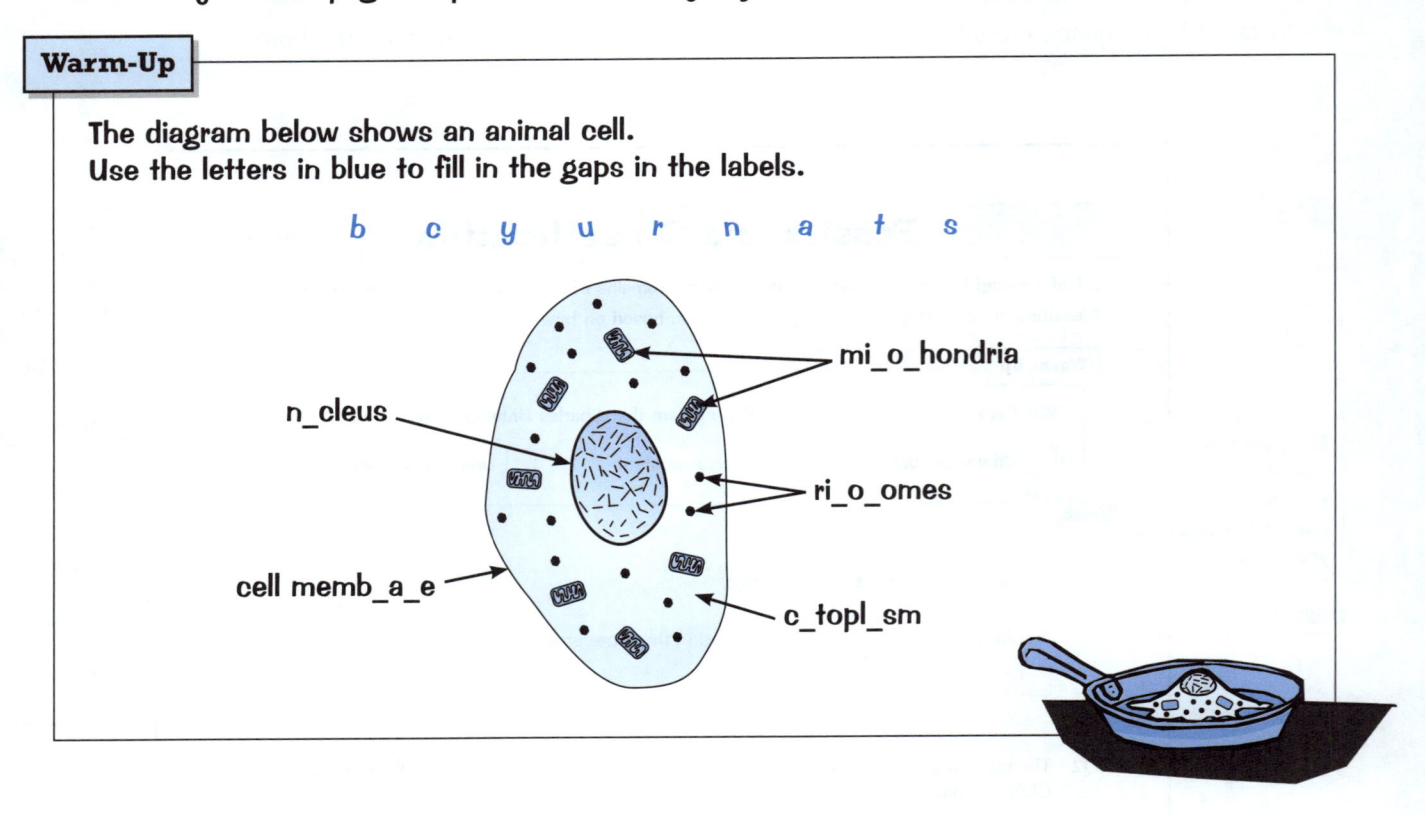

Warm-Up

The diagram below shows an animal cell.
Use the letters in blue to fill in the gaps in the labels.

b   c   y   u   r   n   a   t   s

Labels:
- n_cleus
- mi_o_hondria
- ri_o_omes
- cell memb_a_e
- c_topl_sm

Q1 Circle the words in blue to make these sentences correct.

Plant cells and **animal / bacterial** cells have cell walls. They provide **support / energy** to cells.

Plant cells also have **chloroplasts / plasmids**. These are where photosynthesis happens.

Q2 Which of these is smaller than a bacterial cell?

☐ an animal cell   ☐ a plant cell   ☐ a plasmid   ☐ a hamster

Q3 Fill in the table to show which subcellular structures are being described. They're all found in animal cells.

Subcellular structures are the parts inside cells.

Description	Subcellular structure
Stores genetic material that controls what the cell does.	
Controls what goes in and out of the cell.	
Aerobic respiration happens here.	

Topic B1 — Cell Biology

Q4 Are the following statements true or false?

	True	False
An electron microscope gives a more detailed view of a cell than a light microscope does.	☐	☐
A light microscope has a higher magnification than an electron microscope.	☐	☐

Q5 Where is DNA found in a bacterial cell?

....

....

Q6 Jaime is using a light microscope to study a cell.

The magnification of Jaime's microscope is ×100.
The size of the cell in the image is 5 mm.
Calculate the real size of the cell using the equation below.

$$\text{real size} = \frac{\text{image size}}{\text{magnification}}$$

Real size = ... mm

NOW TRY THIS

You almost need a microscope to see this...

When you use a microscope you'll need to draw what you can see. You can't be too creative though — there's a set of rules you need to follow to make sure your drawing is scientific.

1) Julia has prepared a slide with a layer of garlic cells on it.
   She looks at it under a microscope and draws what she can see.

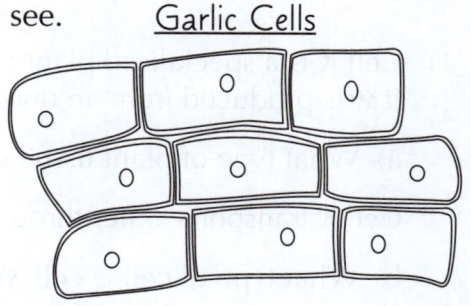

   Garlic Cells

   a) Which of the following statements is true?

      1. Julia should shade each nucleus with a pencil.
      2. Julia should add a scale.
      3. Julia should remove the title.

   b) Suggest one other way that Julia could improve her drawing.

Topic B1 — Cell Biology

Cell Differentiation and Specialisation

The body has lots of different types of cells. The different cells all carry out their own special job (called a function). We call them specialised cells.

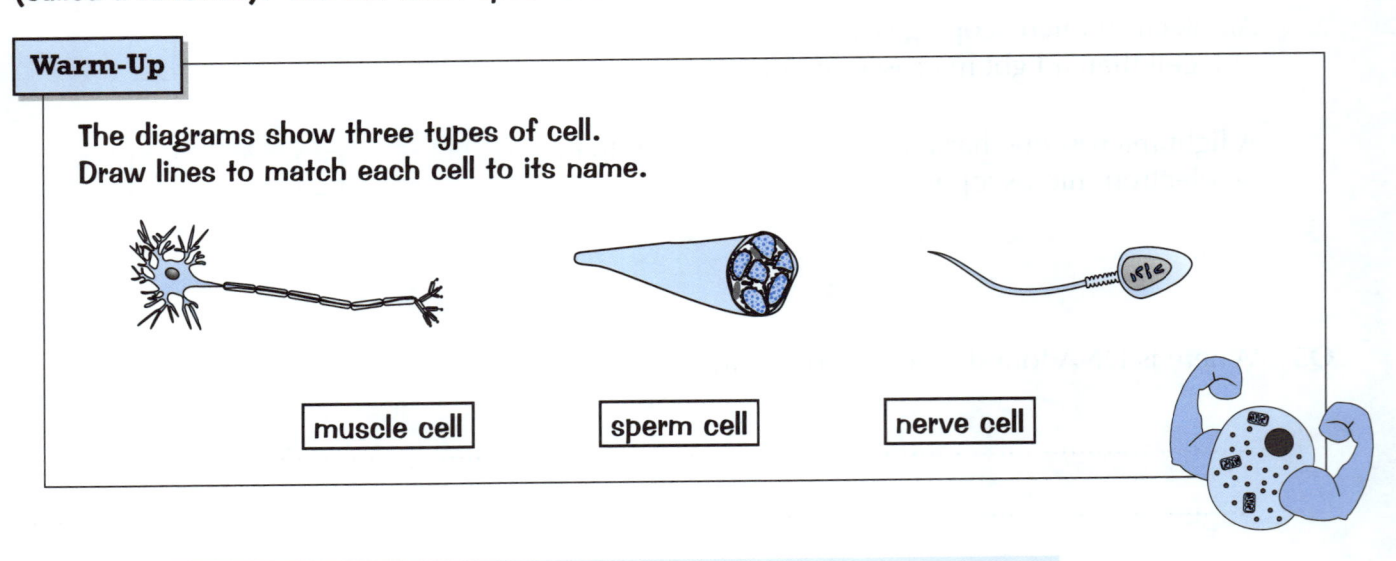

Warm-Up

The diagrams show three types of cell.
Draw lines to match each cell to its name.

muscle cell   sperm cell   nerve cell

Q1 Choose words from the box to fill in the gaps in the paragraph below.

| blood   undifferentiated   embryos   marrow |

Stem cells are .... cells. In human adults, stem cells can be

found in bone .... These stem cells only turn into certain

types of specialised cells, including .... cells. However, human

.... have stem cells that can turn into any type of body cell.

Q2 Give one reason why adults need to produce new specialised cells.

....

Specialisation is my specialist subject...

During differentiation, a cell changes into a different type of cell that has a specific function. It will often develop new subcellular structures so it can carry out this function.

1) Cell X is a specialised plant cell.
   It was produced from an undifferentiated cell.

   a) What type of plant tissue was Cell X produced from?

   Cell X transports water through the plant.

   b) What type of cell is cell X?

   c) Give one way that the structure of the Cell X helps it to do its job.

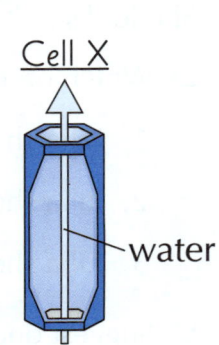

Topic B1 — Cell Biology

Chromosomes and Mitosis

Your body always needs to make new cells. It does this using mitosis.

Warm-Up

Circle the words in blue to make these sentences correct.

Chromosomes are coiled up DNA / protein molecules.

Chromosomes are found in the cytoplasm / nucleus.

Body cells usually have two / three copies of each chromosome.

Each chromosome carries a small / large number of genes.

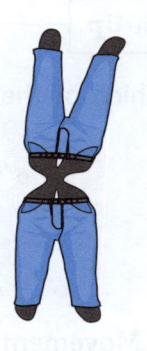

Q1 Are the following statements about mitosis true or false?

	True	False
Mitosis is the stage in the cell cycle where a cell divides.	☐	☐
The cells produced by mitosis have different DNA compared to the original cell.	☐	☐
Organisms use mitosis to grow.	☐	☐

Q2 The diagram shows one stage in the cell cycle. What is happening during this stage?

☐ The cytoplasm and cell membrane are dividing.

☐ The DNA is being copied.

☐ The arms of each chromosome are being pulled apart.

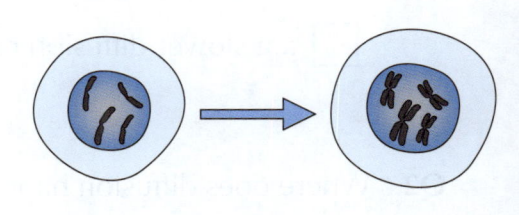

NOW TRY THIS

Learning about mitosis is fun — that's sure to divide opinion...

Before a cell divides, it produces more subcellular structures. Remember, subcellular structures are the parts inside cells, such as mitochondria and ribosomes.

1) The table shows how the number of mitochondria in a cell changes during the cell cycle.

   a) What was the increase in the number of mitochondria between hours 0 to 10?

   b) Suggest why the cell needs to increase its number of mitochondria during the cell cycle.

Time (hours)	Number of mitochondria
0	480
10	600
20	920

Topic B1 — Cell Biology

Transport in Cells

Cells aren't sealed shut — things are always moving between them and their surroundings. There are three ways that this can happen — diffusion, osmosis and active transport.

Warm-Up

Which of these involves osmosis? Circle your answer.

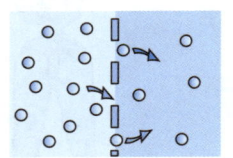

Movement of glucose into a cell

Movement of water into pieces of carrot

Movement of a rake towards Gerald's face

Q1 Tick a box to complete each sentence.

Diffusion is the spreading out of particles...

☐ ...from an area of higher concentration to an area of lower concentration.

☐ ...from an area of lower concentration to an area of higher concentration.

A higher temperature will give...

☐ ...a slower diffusion rate.   ☐ ...a faster diffusion rate.

Q2 Where does diffusion happen? Tick **two** boxes.

☐ in solutions   ☐ in gases   ☐ in solids

Q3 Choose words from the box to fill in the gaps in the sentences below.

| blood | energy | concentration | mineral |

Active transport moves substances against the .... gradient.

It needs .... from respiration to happen. Active transport is

used by plant root hair cells to absorb .... ions from the soil.

Active transport also happens in animals. For example, it allows glucose to

be transported from the gut into the ....

Topic B1 — Cell Biology

Q4 Which of these has the largest surface area to volume ratio?

☐ an elephant ☐ a human ☐ a bacterium

Q5 A snake has a surface area of 1000 cm². Its volume is 200 cm³. What is its surface area to volume ratio?

$\frac{1000}{200}$ = ...

So its surface area to volume ratio is .... : 1

Q6 Roots are covered in root hairs, as shown in the diagram. How does the structure of root hairs help them absorb as much water from the soil as possible?

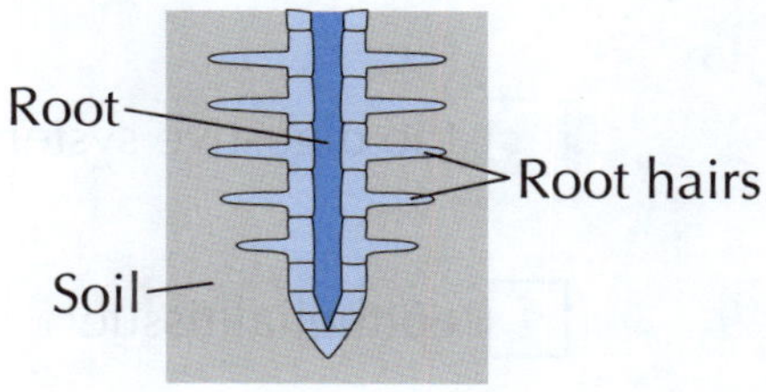

....
....
....
....

Water diffuses into plant roots from the soil.

Water and criminals — things that get transported into cells...

NOW TRY THIS

Osmosis is pretty similar to diffusion. In fact, osmosis is just a special type of diffusion — it's the diffusion of water across a partially permeable membrane.

1) Sean weighs a potato cylinder. He then places it in a salty solution. The next day, Sean dries the cylinder and weighs it again. His results are shown in the table.

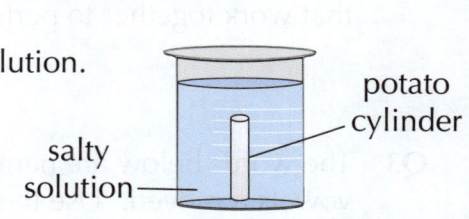

   a) Calculate the percentage loss of mass from the cylinder. Use the equation below:

   percentage loss = $\frac{\text{mass at the start} - \text{mass at the end}}{\text{mass at the start}} \times 100$

Mass at the start (g)	Mass at the end (g)
6.0	4.5

   b) Has water moved **into** the cylinder or **out of** the cylinder?

   c) Why has the water moved in this direction?

Topic B1 — Cell Biology

Topic B2 — Organisation

Cell Organisation in Animals and Plants

All living things are made of cells. Trees, fish, rabbits, your brother, your brother's rabbit... basically everything. You need to know how cells are organised in animals and plants.

Warm-Up

Tick whether each sentence is true or false.

	True	False
Cells are smaller than tissues.	☐	☐
Tissues are made up of organs.	☐	☐
The leaf is a plant organ.	☐	☐

Q1 Which of these is an organ system?

☐ the digestive system ☐ the stomach

☐ epithelial tissue ☐ a piano

Q2 Choose words from the box to fill in the gaps in the paragraph below.

> tissues   function   organs   cells

A tissue is a group of similar .... that work together to carry out a

particular .... An organ is a group of different ....

that work together to perform a function. .... make up organ systems.

Q3 The words below are names of plant tissues, with the vowels removed. Use the clues to figure out the words.

This is found at the growing tips of shoots and roots.   m__r__st__m

This covers the whole plant.   __p__d__rm__l

This helps to transport substances around the plant.   xyl__m

Q4 Draw lines to match each plant tissue with the letter that shows its position on the diagram and its function (job).

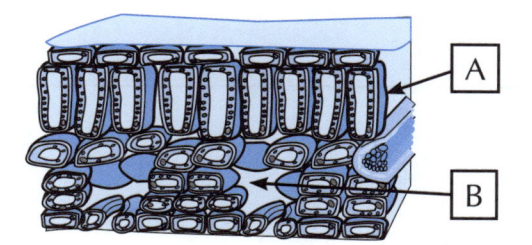

| A | palisade mesophyll | contains big air spaces so that gases can diffuse |
| B | spongy mesophyll | most photosynthesis happens here |

Q5 Circle the words in blue to make these sentences correct.

Stomata / chloroplasts let gases diffuse into and out of a leaf.

They are opened and closed in response to the **environment / leaf's feelings**.

This is controlled by the **guard cells / meristem**.

Q6 Name two organs that are found in the digestive system.

1. ....

2. ....

NOW TRY THIS

Time to see how organised your learning has been...

Cells need to be organised so that everything in the organism works as it should.
Your notes need to be organised so that you learn everything that you need to know.

1) The circulatory system is made up of different organs that work together to transport blood all over the body. The heart and the lungs are two of the organs in the circulatory system.

   a) What is the circulatory system an example of?

      1. a cell
      2. a tissue
      3. an organ system

   The heart is made of heart muscle. Heart muscle is made of smaller building blocks.

   b) Is heart muscle a tissue or an organ?

   c) What are the smaller building blocks that the heart muscle is made of?

Topic B2 — Organisation

Enzymes

We have loads and loads of reactions going on all the time in our cells.
Enzymes make these reactions work. Fancy that.

Warm-Up

The diagram shows a model of how enzymes work.

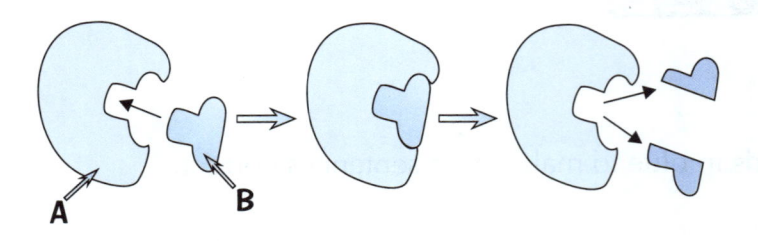

What is the name of the model?

☐ the lock and key model   ☐ the substrate model   ☐ the magic model

Which label is pointing to the enzyme?

☐ A   ☐ B

Q1 Tick whether each sentence is true or false.

	True	False
Enzymes speed up reactions.	☐	☐
Enzymes get used up in reactions.	☐	☐

Q2 Choose words from the box to fill in the gaps in the paragraph below.

active   fit   unique   one

Every enzyme has an .... site. This site has a .... shape.

The substance involved in the reaction has to .... into the active site for the

enzyme to work. This means that enzymes only catalyse .... specific reaction.

Topic B2 — Organisation

Q3 The graph shows the rate of an enzyme reaction at different pHs.
Which part of the graph shows the pH that the enzyme works best at?

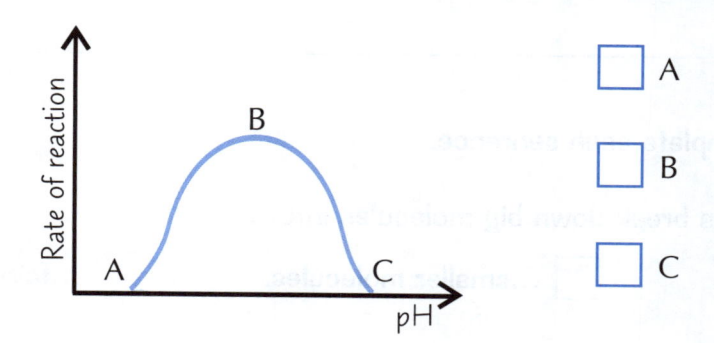

☐ A
☐ B
☐ C

Q4 Circle the words in blue to make these sentences correct.

The enzyme **amylase / iodine** breaks down starch into **sugar / protein**.

You can detect starch using **amylase / iodine** solution. If starch is present, this solution

will change from **browny-orange / blue-black** to **browny-orange / blue-black**.

Q5 If an enzyme gets too hot, it will change shape.
Why does this mean it will stop working?

....

....

NOW TRY THIS

I stop working when the sun comes out too...

Goldilocks liked the temperature of her porridge to be just right — not too hot, not too cold. Enzymes work best when their temperature (and pH) is just right too.

1) Samia is investigating the effect of pH on enzyme activity. She places one drop of iodine into each dimple on a spotting tile. She adds amylase to a starch solution. Every ten seconds she removes a sample of the starch-amylase solution and adds it to a dimple on the spotting tile.

   a) How will Samia know when all the starch has been broken down?

   b) Temperature affects enzyme activity.
   Why must Samia control the temperature of the reaction?

   c) How could Samia control the temperature of the reaction?

   d) It takes 80 seconds for the amylase to break down all of the starch.
   Use the equation below to calculate the rate of reaction.
   The units are s^{-1}.

   $$\text{Rate} = \frac{1000}{\text{time}}$$

Topic B2 — Organisation

Digestion and Food Tests

Every time you have a bite to eat, your digestive enzymes work to break down the food.

Warm-Up

Tick a box to complete each sentence.

Digestive enzymes break down big molecules into...

☐ ...enzymes.   ☐ ...smaller molecules.   ☐ ...fairy dust.

For example, proteins are broken down into...

☐ ...sugars.   ☐ ...glycerol.   ☐ ...amino acids.

Q1 Circle the words in blue to make these sentences correct.

Carbohydrases break down **carbohydrates / proteins** into **sugars / amino acids**.

An example of a carbohydrase is **protease / amylase**.

This enzyme is produced in the **stomach / salivary glands**.

Q2 Draw lines to match each solution below to the molecules it can be used to test for.

Benedict's solution	sugars
iodine solution	proteins
biuret solution	starch

Q3 The words below are names of digestive enzymes, with some of the vowels removed. Use the clues to figure out the words.

This enzyme is used to break down starch.   __myl__s__

These enzymes are used to break down proteins.   pr__te__ses

These enzymes are used to break down lipids.   l__pas__s

Lipids are fats and oils.

Topic B2 — Organisation

Q4 Are the following statements true or false? Tick the correct boxes.

	True	False
Lipids are broken down into sugars and fatty acids.	☐	☐
The products of digestion can be used to make new carbohydrates, proteins and lipids.	☐	☐
Some of the glucose produced by digestion is used in respiration.	☐	☐
Proteases work in the stomach and small intestine.	☐	☐
Starch molecules can be absorbed straight into the bloodstream.	☐	☐

Q5 Name two places in the body where lipases are produced.

1. ....

2. ....

Crumbs — all that was left after the cake had been broken down...

NOW TRY THIS

Biologists love doing experiments to see what is in their food.
As for me, I'm happy just eating my food. Takes all sorts I suppose.

1) William wants to find out if the beef in his burger contains glucose.
   He prepares a sample of the beef to test.

   a) William adds a solution to his beef sample to test for glucose.
      The solution stays bright blue. Is there glucose in William's beef sample?

   William decides to test his beef sample for protein.
   He adds a solution to his beef sample to test for proteins.

   b) He finds that his beef sample does contain protein.
      What colour change happened in the solution for him to conclude this?

   c) Suggest a safety precaution that William needs to take in his experiment.

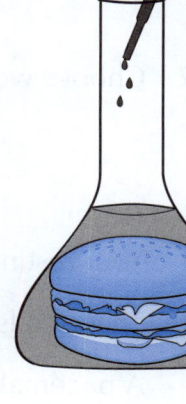

Topic B2 — Organisation

The Lungs and the Heart

The structures of the lungs and the heart are a little complicated. Take some time to learn them.

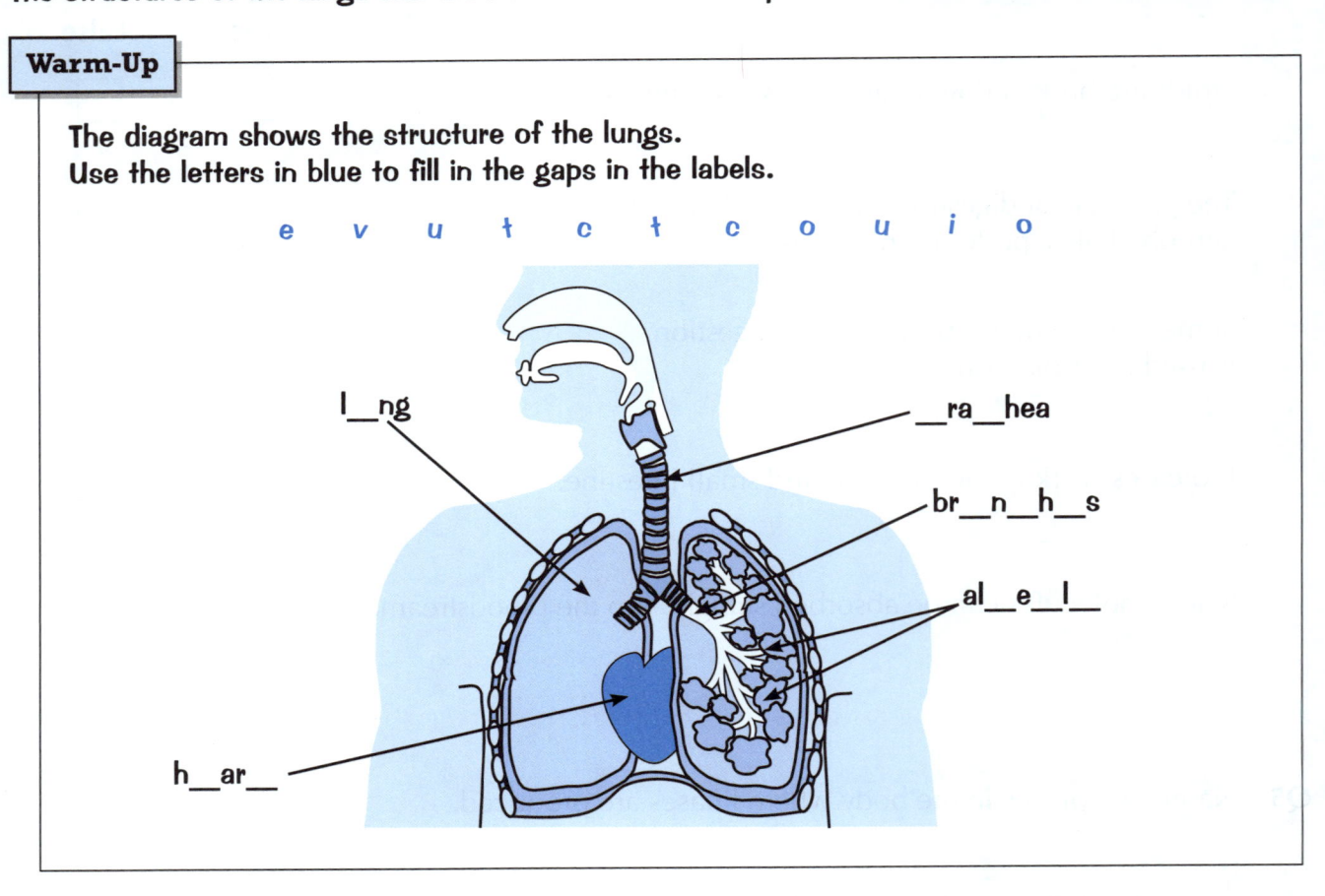

Warm-Up

The diagram shows the structure of the lungs.
Use the letters in blue to fill in the gaps in the labels.

e   v   u   t   c   t   c   o   u   i   o

- l_ng
- __ra__hea
- br__n__h__s
- al__e__l__
- h__ar__

Q1 The diagram shows the structure of the heart.

Which letter shows the left ventricle?
☐ A   ☐ B   ☐ C

Which letter shows the right ventricle?
☐ A   ☐ B   ☐ C

Q2 Choose words from the box to fill in the gaps in the paragraph below.

| atrium | heart | irregular | pump |

Your resting .... rate is controlled by a group of cells in the right ....

These cells act as a pacemaker — they tell the heart when to .... blood.

A pacemaker that doesn't work properly causes an .... heartbeat.

Topic B2 — Organisation

Q3 The diagram shows a part of the lungs where gas exchange takes place.
What are the names of structures X and Y?

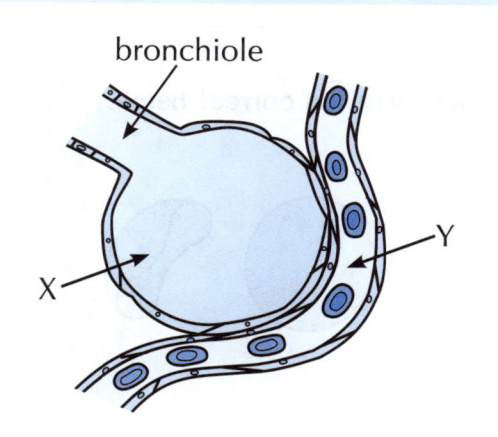

bronchiole

Structure X is an ....

Structure Y is a ....

Q4 Tick a box to complete each sentence.

Blood from the heart's right ventricle...

☐ ...goes through the pulmonary artery to the lungs.

☐ ...goes through the aorta to the rest of the body.

Blood from the heart's left ventricle...

☐ ...goes through the pulmonary artery to the lungs.

☐ ...goes through the aorta to the rest of the body.

Beans, beans, are good for the heart, the more you eat the more you...

...never mind. The circulatory system is super important. It gets food molecules and oxygen to every cell in your body. It also takes all the waste away. Neat.

1) The diagrams show a single circulatory system and a double circulatory system.

   a) Which diagram (A or B) shows a double circulatory system?

   b) Give one difference between the double circulatory system and the single circulatory system.

   c) The blood vessel labelled X on diagram A returns blood to the heart from the rest of the body.
   What is the name of blood vessel X?

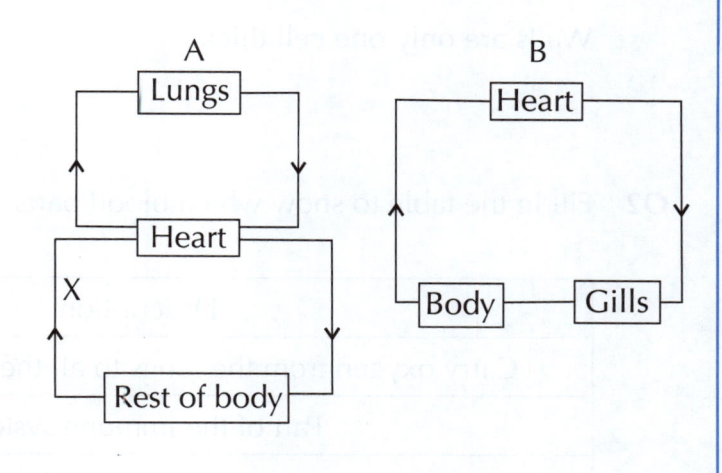

A: Lungs → Heart → Rest of body (X)

B: Heart → Body → Gills

Topic B2 — Organisation

Blood and Blood Vessels

There are three different types of blood vessel. They carry blood around your body. Simple.

Warm-Up

Draw lines to match the pictures of different blood parts with the correct name. One has been done for you.

red blood cells | white blood cells | platelets

Q1 These facts are about blood vessels. For each one, tick whether it is true for arteries, capillaries or veins.

	Arteries	Capillaries	Veins
Carry blood back to the heart at low pressure.	☐	☐	☐
Carry blood away from the heart at high pressure.	☐	☐	☐
Carry blood really close to every cell in the body to exchange substances with them.	☐	☐	☐
Walls are only one cell thick.	☐	☐	☐

Q2 Fill in the table to show which blood parts are being described.

Description	Blood part
Carry oxygen from the lungs to all the cells in the body.	
Part of the immune system.	
Help blood to clot.	

Topic B2 — Organisation

Q3 Circle the words in blue to make these sentences correct.

Plasma is a **liquid / gas** that carries everything in blood.

For example, it carries red blood cells, hormones and **proteins / chocolate** .

Q4 1625 cm³ of blood flows through an artery in 5 minutes. Use the equation below to calculate the rate of blood flow through the artery in cm³ per minute.

$$\text{rate of blood flow} = \frac{\text{volume of blood}}{\text{number of minutes}}$$

rate of blood flow = ... cm³ per minute

Q5 Give two ways that the structure of an artery is suited to its function (job).

1. ....
   ....
2. ....
   ....

Always give 100% — unless you're giving blood...

NOW TRY THIS

Blood is an important tissue. It transports substances all around your body. Make sure you know the structure and function of each type of blood vessel.

1) A scientist is studying the structure of the blood vessels in a horse. Like humans, horses have arteries, capillaries and veins.

   a) The scientist looks at one of the horse's blood vessels under a microscope. She sees that it contains valves. What type of blood vessel is she looking at?

   b) The diagram shows two cross-sections of blood vessels from the horse. Which one (X or Y) is the vein? How do you know?

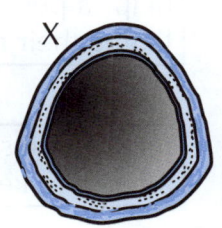

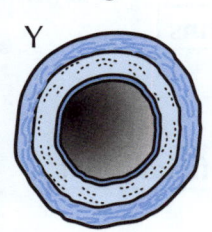

Topic B2 — Organisation

Health and Disease

Disease isn't a fun thing to think about. There are a few things you need to learn though. Best get cracking with these questions...

Warm-Up

Which of these sentences is true?

☐ Health depends only on how physically healthy you are.

☐ Health depends only on how mentally healthy you are.

☐ Health is a state of both physical and mental wellbeing.

Q1 Circle the words in blue to make these sentences correct.

Cancer is caused by **uncontrolled / controlled** cell growth and division.

Lifestyle factors, like smoking, can **increase / decrease** the chance of some cancers.

Q2 Choose words from the box to fill in the gaps in the paragraph below.

| reduces | coronary | narrow | fatty |

Coronary heart disease is a disease of the .... arteries.

Layers of .... material build up in these arteries. This causes the arteries to become .... This .... blood flow to the heart muscle.

Q3 Draw lines to match each treatment for coronary heart disease with its function.

| stents | | drugs that reduce the amount of cholesterol in the blood |

Cholesterol is a type of fat.

| statins | | helps a person recover by letting their heart rest and heal |

| artificial heart | | tubes put inside the coronary arteries to keep them open |

Topic B2 — Organisation

Q4 Are the following statements true or false?

	True	False
Risk factors increase your chance of getting a disease.	☐	☐
Having risk factors for a disease means that you will definitely get a disease.	☐	☐
Viruses infect cells in the body. This can lead to some types of cancer.	☐	☐
Substances in a person's environment do not increase their chance of getting a disease.	☐	☐
Obesity is a risk factor for Type 2 diabetes.	☐	☐

Q5 Diseases can be communicable or non-communicable. What is a non-communicable disease?

....
....
....

NOW TRY THIS

GCSE Science revision — a risk factor for brain frazzle...

Make sure you understand how different diseases can interact. For example, a person may become depressed if they can't carry out everyday activities because they are ill.

1) Ruben has a bad cold. He is coughing and sneezing. His sister Pearl looks after Ruben while he is sick. Soon after Pearl becomes unwell too.

   a) What kind of disease does Ruben have?

      1. communicable   2. non-communicable

   b) Pearl has asthma. Why could it be dangerous for Pearl to catch Ruben's cold?

   Ruben and Pearl's mum has a very stressful job. She eats a lot of fast food because she doesn't have time to cook healthy meals.

   c) Suggest two lifestyle factors that could affect their mum's health.

Topic B2 — Organisation

Transpiration and Translocation

Transpiration is the movement of water through the plant.
Translocation is the movement of food molecules through the plant.

Warm-Up

Which one of these does not affect the rate of transpiration? Circle your answer.

Air flow    Light intensity    What you had for lunch

Q1 Phloem and xylem are plant tissues. For each of the facts below, decide whether it is true for phloem or xylem. Write your answers under the correct heading in the table.

Transports sugars around the plant.

Transports water around the plant.

Transports mineral ions around the plant.

Transports substances from the leaves to other parts of the plant.

Phloem	Xylem

Q2 The words below are substances or structures in plants. Some letters are missing. Use the clues to figure out the words.

Strengthens the walls in xylem tubes.   l__gn__n

Liquid that flows through phloem tubes.   c__ll s__p

Small holes in the end walls of phloem cells.   p__r__s

Topic B2 — Organisation

Q3 Choose words from the box to fill in the gaps in the paragraph below.

| diffuses | xylem | stream | roots |

Water evaporates from the leaves and .... into the air.

More water is drawn up from the rest of the plant through the .... tubes

to replace it. This means that more water is drawn up from the ....

The movement of water through the plant is called the transpiration ....

Q4 Draw lines to complete the sentences.

Stomata are tiny pores in the surface of the leaf.

| The stomata close so that... | ...gases can be exchanged for photosynthesis. |

| When the stomata are open... | ...because stomata close when it gets dark. |

| The transpiration rate is very low at night... | ...water vapour can't escape from the plant. |

Just one call moves food from my local takeaway to my stomach...

NOW TRY THIS

Transpiration and translocation are two fancy words for two very important processes. They move water and food around the plant so that everything ends up where it needs to be.

1) The graph shows the rate of transpiration in a plant against temperature.

   a) Which part of the graph (A or B) shows the rate of transpiration increasing?

   b) Which of these statements is true?

   1. At high temperatures the rate of transpiration decreases.
   2. At high temperatures the rate of transpiration stays the same.
   3. At high temperatures the rate of transpiration increases faster.

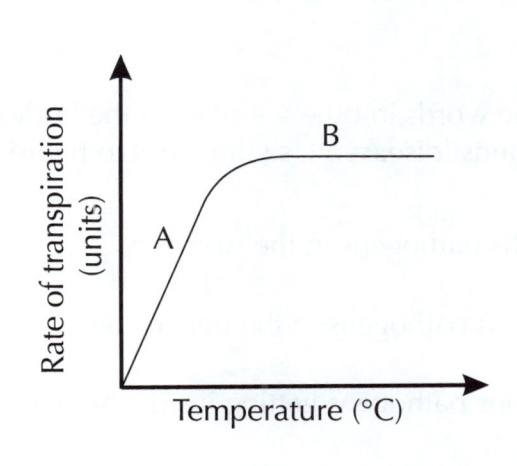

Topic B2 — Organisation

Topic B3 — Infection and Response

Pathogens and the Immune System

Pathogens are microorganisms that cause disease. Thankfully, our bodies fight them off.

Warm-Up

Which <u>two</u> of these could be pathogens? Circle your answers.

a wasp   a bacterium   a goose   a virus

Q1 Are these statements true or false?

	True	False
Pathogens only infect animals.	☐	☐
Some fungi are pathogens.	☐	☐
Some pathogens can be spread in the air.	☐	☐

Q2 What is a communicable disease? Circle the answer.

Communicable diseases are also known as infectious diseases.

A disease that can be spread

A disease caused by faulty DNA

A disease that only affects plants

A disease that can talk to other diseases

Q3 The words in blue are parts of the body's defence system against disease. Use the clues to figure out the words.

Kills pathogens in the stomach.   stomach __c__d

Traps pathogens in the trachea and bronchi.   m__cu__

Stops pathogens getting inside the body.   s__i__

Topic B3 — Infection and Response

Q4 Draw lines to match each word to the correct description.

White blood cells	When cells in the immune system surround and digest pathogens.
Antibodies	Cells that destroy pathogens.
Phagocytosis	Molecules that lock on to invading pathogens.

Q5 Circle the words in blue to make these sentences correct.

Antibodies are made by **red / white** blood cells. These cells start making antibodies when they come across a pathogen's **antigens / antitoxins**.

One antibody works on **one type / all types** of pathogen.

Q6 How do antitoxins help to protect the body from bacteria?

....
....

Q7 A pathogen is spread by water. How could you get infected with this pathogen?

....
....

NOW TRY THIS

I'll never take my white blood cells for granted again...

People can reduce the spread of disease in different ways.
How you do it depends on things like how the disease is spread.

1) Chickenpox is a disease that can be spread by coughs and sneezes.

   a) Suggest one way of reducing the spread of chickenpox.

   Norovirus is a pathogen that can be spread by direct contact with infected surfaces.

   b) Suggest one way of reducing the spread of norovirus.

Topic B3 — Infection and Response

Types of Disease

You need to know examples of diseases caused by bacteria, viruses, protists and fungi.

Warm-Up

Which of these could get infected with rose black spot? Circle your answer.

Q1 Tick a box to complete each sentence.

Viruses live and reproduce...

☐ ...inside cells.   ☐ ...outside cells.

Bacteria can make you feel ill by...

☐ ...reproducing rapidly.   ☐ ...producing toxins (poisons).

Q2 Are these statements are true or false? Circle the answers.

People can be vaccinated against measles.	True False
Gonorrhoea can always be cured with the antibiotic penicillin.	True False
Tobacco mosaic virus can only infect tobacco plants.	True False

Q3 Circle the words in blue to make these sentences correct.

HIV attacks the body's **immune / digestive** system.

It causes an illness that is similar to **flu / measles** soon after infecting someone.

An HIV infection can be controlled with **penicillin / antiretroviral drugs** .

If it is not treated, an HIV infection can eventually lead to **malaria / AIDS** .

Topic B3 — Infection and Response

Q4 Draw lines to match each disease to a way it can be spread.

measles — through bites from infected mosquitoes

HIV infection — in droplets from an infected person's sneeze

malaria — by sexual contact

Q5 Is each of these diseases caused by a bacterium, a virus or a protist?

	Bacterium	Virus	Protist
HIV infection	☐	☐	☐
Gonorrhoea	☐	☐	☐
Measles	☐	☐	☐
Malaria	☐	☐	☐
Salmonella	☐	☐	☐

Ella the Salmon

Q6 Give one example of a disease caused by a fungus.

....

NOW TRY THIS

Warning — this book may spread knowledge...

There are seven diseases mentioned on these pages. For each one, try to learn what kind of pathogen causes it, what its symptoms are and how we can stop it spreading.

1) A doctor is treating patients.

   The first patient has pain when he pees. He also has a thick yellow discharge coming from his penis.

   a) Suggest what bacterial disease he might have.

   The second patient has a fever and a red skin rash.

   b) Suggest what viral disease she might have.

Topic B3 — Infection and Response

Drugs

On the last few pages you saw some of the nasty diseases that pathogens can cause.
But here's some good news — many of them can be treated using medicines, such as antibiotics.

Warm-Up

What do antibiotics kill?

☐ viruses   ☐ plants   ☐ bacteria   ☐ aunties

What are painkillers used for?

....

Q1 What is aspirin?

☐ an antibiotic   ☐ a painkiller   ☐ a placebo

Q2 Which antibiotic did Alexander Fleming discover?

....

Q3 The words below are sources of medicine, with some letters removed. Use the clues to figure out the words.

A tree that was used to make aspirin.   w__ll__w

A type of mould that makes penicillin.   Peni__illi__m

A plant that was used to make digitalis.   fox__lo__e

Digitalis is a heart medicine.

Q4 Choose words from the box to fill in the gaps in the paragraph below.

| chemists   pharmaceutical   microorganisms |

Many drugs first came from plants or .... Drugs are now

usually made by .... in laboratories. The companies that make

and sell drugs are part of the .... industry.

Topic B3 — Infection and Response

Q5 The things below need to be done before a new drug can be given to patients. Put them in the right order by writing the numbers 1-3 in the boxes.

☐ Clinical testing is carried out on human volunteers.

☐ A new chemical is discovered that can be used as a drug.

☐ Preclinical testing is carried out on human cells and live animals.

Q6 Use the words in the boxes to fill in the table.

toxicity   efficacy   dosage

Word to do with drug testing	What the word means
	The concentration of the drug that works best and how often it should be taken.
	How harmful the drug is and whether it has any side effects.
	Whether the drug works and has the effect you're looking for.

Q7 Some pathogens are resistant to antibiotics. What does this mean?

....

NOW TRY THIS

If only there was medicine that cured me of laziness...

Antibiotics have saved millions of lives since they were first discovered. Unfortunately, there are still diseases that we haven't found a cure for yet.

1) Farzana has the flu, which is caused by a virus. It's causing pain in her muscles. She takes painkillers to make her feel better.

   a) The painkillers don't get rid of the flu. Explain why.

   b) Farzana's doctor will not give her antibiotics for the flu. Explain why.

Topic B3 — Infection and Response

Topic B4 — Bioenergetics

Photosynthesis

Plants use photosynthesis to make food for themselves.
It happens in all of the green bits of the plant — particularly the leaves.

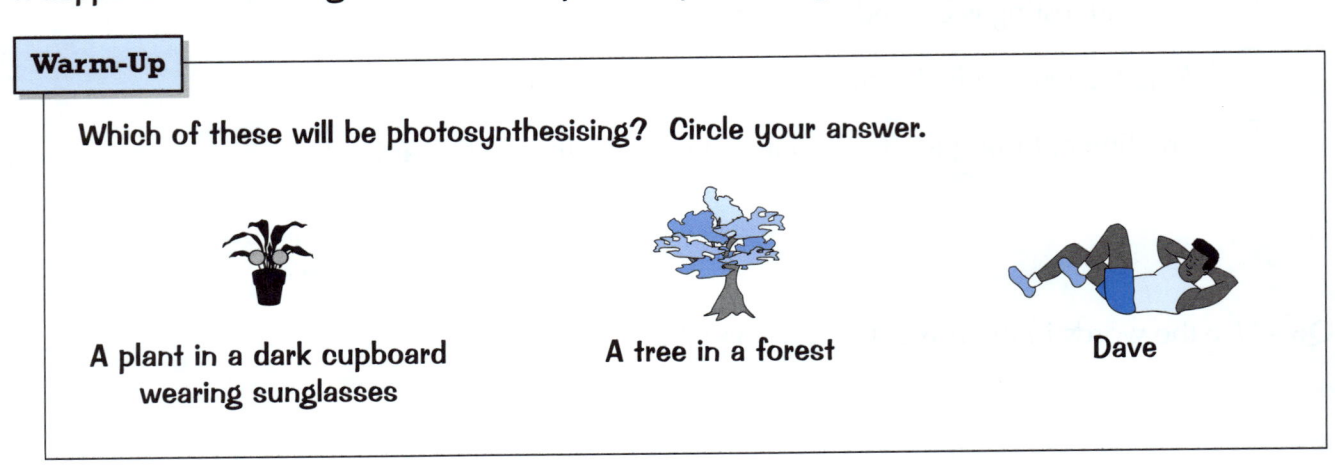

Warm-Up

Which of these will be photosynthesising? Circle your answer.

A plant in a dark cupboard wearing sunglasses

A tree in a forest

Dave

Q1 Circle the words in blue to make these sentences correct.

Photosynthesis happens in plant cells in structures called **mitochondria / chloroplasts**.

These contain a chemical called **chlorophyll / cellulose**.

Photosynthesis is an **endothermic / exothermic** reaction.

Endothermic means energy is transferred from the environment. Exothermic means energy is transferred to the environment.

Q2 The words below are things plants make from glucose, with the vowels removed. Use the clues to figure out the words.

This is an energy store made from glucose.	st__rch	*There are two vowels missing here.*
These are also energy stores.	f__ts and ____ls	
This is what makes cell walls strong.	c__ll__l__s__	
Proteins are made up of these.	__m__n__ __c__ds	

Energy Store — Half price sale today!

Q3 What is the word equation for photosynthesis? Use the words below to fill in the gaps.

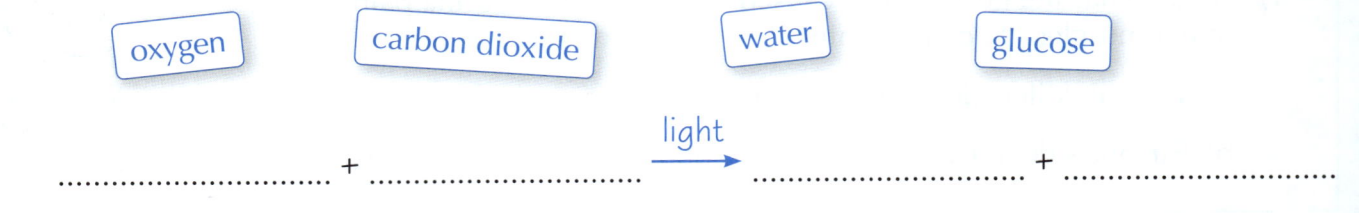

oxygen   carbon dioxide   water   glucose

.... + ... →(light) .... + ...

Q4 A limiting factor is something that affects how quickly a plant can photosynthesise. Which one of these is a limiting factor for photosynthesis?

☐ the amount of chlorophyll in the plant's leaves

☐ the amount of nitrogen in the air

☐ the amount of water in the soil

☐ how much coffee the plant has drunk

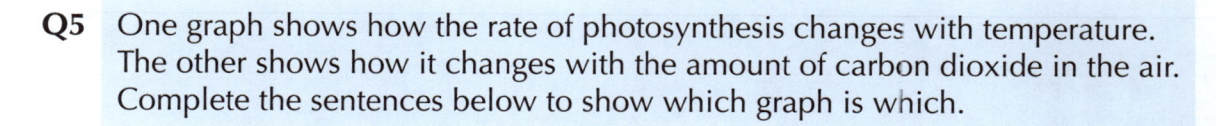

Q5 One graph shows how the rate of photosynthesis changes with temperature. The other shows how it changes with the amount of carbon dioxide in the air. Complete the sentences below to show which graph is which.

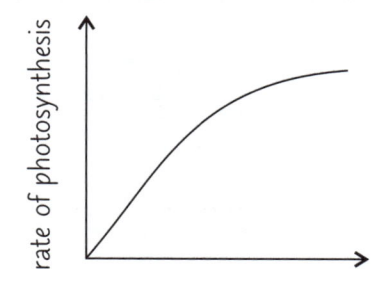

How the rate of photosynthesis changes with

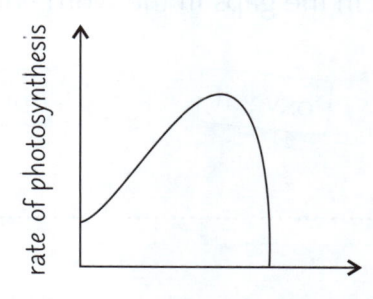

....

How the rate of photosynthesis changes with

....

Time for a photo finish...

NOW TRY THIS

Biologists love doing experiments with pondweed and lamps.
I love chilling on the sofa with a can of pop. Everyone's different, I guess.

1) Janey measures the rate of photosynthesis of pondweed at different light intensities. She uses the equipment shown on the right.

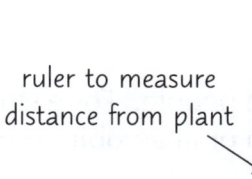

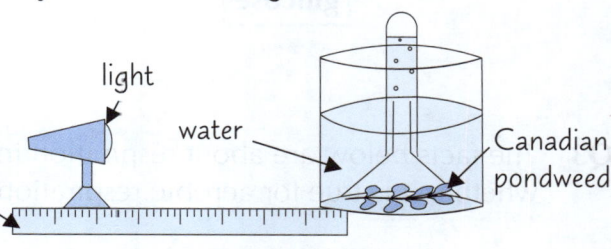

Janey varies the light intensity by moving the lamp away from the pondweed. She counts how many bubbles the pondweed gives off in one minute at each distance.

a) What gas is in the bubbles?

The graph on the right shows Janey's results.

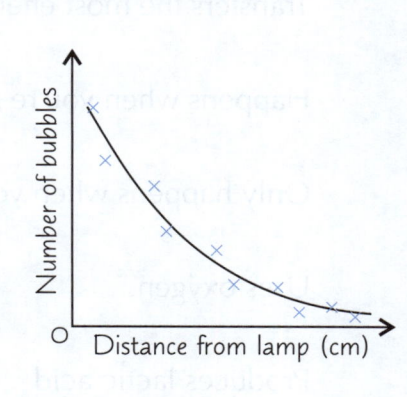

b) Does the number of bubbles increase or decrease as distance from the lamp increases?

c) What does your answer to b) tell you about how the rate of photosynthesis changes as distance from the lamp increases?

d) What is causing the rate of photosynthesis to change?

Topic B4 — Bioenergetics

Respiration and Exercise

Respiration is how you get the energy to do anything. Talking, dancing, answering science questions... basically everything. There are two different types you need to know about.

Warm-Up

Respiration transfers ....

It happens in: ☐ cells   ☐ the Sun   ☐ comic books

Q1 Fill in the gaps in the word equation for aerobic respiration. Use the words below.

oxygen   carbon dioxide   water   glucose

.... + ... → .... + ...

Q2 Draw lines to match the names of the chemicals with their symbols.

water $C_6H_{12}O_6$

carbon dioxide CO_2

glucose H_2O

Q3 The facts below are about respiration in people. For each fact, tick whether it is true for aerobic respiration or anaerobic respiration.

	aerobic	anaerobic
Transfers the most energy.	☐	☐
Happens when you're sitting at your desk.	☐	☐
Only happens when you exercise hard.	☐	☐
Uses oxygen.	☐	☐
Produces lactic acid.	☐	☐

Topic B4 — Bioenergetics

Q4 Circle the words in blue to make these sentences correct.

When you exercise, your breathing rate and breath volume **increase / decrease** .

This **increases / decreases** the amount of oxygen in your blood.

Q5 Fill in the crossword using the clues. Some letters have been filled in for you.

Across

3) The chemical with the symbol O₂ (6)

5) Something you use the energy from respiration for (8)

6) You use energy from respiration to stay this way (4)

7) You make this when you exercise hard (6,4)

Down

1) The type of respiration where glucose isn't broken down completely (9)

2) This is an organism that respires to make alcohol in beer and wine (5)

4) A food made using 2 down (it makes a good sandwich) (5)

Q6 Write the word equation for anaerobic respiration in plant cells.

....

Phew — I needed all my energy for that crossword...

NOW TRY THIS

You're not quite done yet, I'm afraid. Now you know the facts, have a go at applying them.

1) Sami and Nish have a similar level of fitness. They wear heart rate monitors while doing some exercise. The graph shows their heart rate over time.

   a) Whose heart rate increased the most?

   b) One of Sami and Nish was running and the other was jogging. From the graph, which do you think was which? Explain your answer.

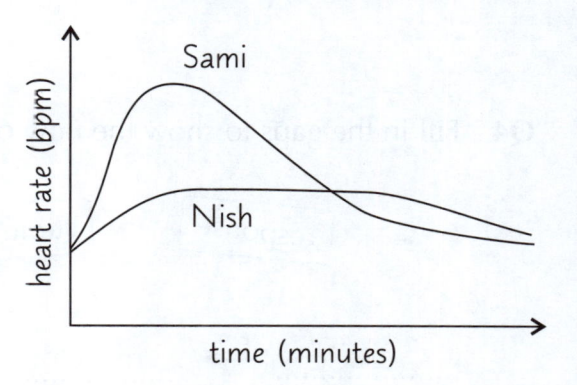

Topic B4 — Bioenergetics

Topic B5 — Homeostasis and Response

Homeostasis and the Nervous System

When changes happen outside your body, homeostasis keeps everything steady inside your body.

Warm-Up

Which of these is not controlled by homeostasis? Circle your answer.

body temperature   water levels (in the body)   the weather

Q1 Tick whether each sentence is true or false.

	True	False
Control systems in homeostasis are automatic.	☐	☐
Control systems in homeostasis only involve nervous responses.	☐	☐

Automatic means you don't have to think about them.

Q2 Which of these is a coordination centre? Circle **two** answers.

the nose   the pancreas   the big toenail
        the brain   the knee

Q3 The words below are to do with control systems. Draw lines to match them to the correct descriptions.

stimulus — a cell that detects changes in the environment

effector — a change in the environment

receptor — a muscle or gland that brings about a response

Q4 Fill in the gaps to show the flow of information through the nervous system.

response   stimulus   effector   CNS

The CNS is the Central Nervous System.

.... → receptor → .... → .... → ....

Topic B5 — Homeostasis and Response

Reflexes and Reaction Time

Reflexes are a type of reaction. They are controlled by the nervous system.
Information in reflexes travels as electrical (nervous) impulses along cells called neurones.

Warm-Up

Underline the sentence that is true.

You don't have to think about reflexes.

Reflexes are quite slow.

Q1 Write numbers in the boxes to show the order of neurones in a reflex.

☐ motor neurone ☐ sensory neurone ☐ relay neurone

Q2 Complete this sentence.

Reflex actions are important because ....

Q3 The diagram shows a synapse.
How does a nervous impulse get across the synapse?

☐ It jumps across the gap.

☐ Chemicals move across the gap and set off a new impulse in the next neurone.

Boredom — my reaction to all this learning...

Reaction time is the time it takes to respond to a stimulus. When my alarm rings in the morning, it takes me a while to react. But if I saw a tiger, I'd be away in a flash.

1) A computer test is used to measure a student's reaction time.
The student has to click when a light turns from red to green.

The test was repeated three times. The mean reaction time was 255 ms.

a) How could you calculate a mean reaction time from three repeat results?

The student drinks a large cup of coffee. After 10 minutes he repeats the experiment.
His mean reaction time is 210 ms.

b) Did the coffee speed up or slow down the student's reaction time?

Topic B5 — Homeostasis and Response

Hormones and Controlling Blood Glucose

Hormones are chemicals that are released by glands in the body. They control all sorts of things.

Warm-Up

Circle three glands in the human body.

thyroid   thumb   testes   ovaries   shoulder   ear

Q1 Circle the words in blue to make these sentences correct.

Hormones travel **in the blood / as electrical impulses**.

Hormones have a **slower / faster** action than nerves.

Hormones act for a **longer / shorter** time than nerves.

Q2 The diagram shows some glands in the human body.

Colour in the gland that produces insulin.

What is the name of the gland that produces insulin?

....

Circle the 'master gland'.

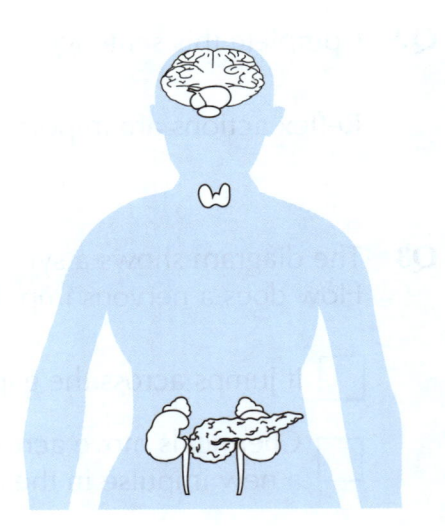

Hormones are like tortoises — slow but steady...

NOW TRY THIS

Hormones are chemical messengers. They only affect particular cells in particular organs. These organs are called target organs.

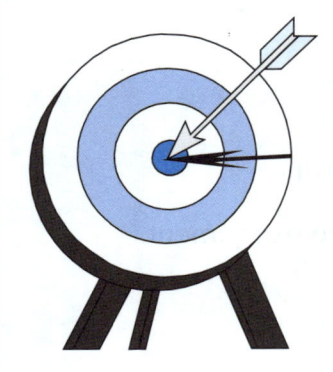

1) Malika eats a slice of chocolate cake. Shortly afterwards, her body releases insulin into her blood.

   a) Why does her body release insulin?

   b) What happens in Malika's muscle cells when insulin is released?

   c) Apart from muscles, name another target organ of insulin.

   d) Malika's brother Issac has a condition where his cells don't respond to the insulin he produces. What is the name of this condition?

Topic B5 — Homeostasis and Response

Puberty and the Menstrual Cycle

At puberty, the release of reproductive hormones causes changes in the body. In women, the menstrual cycle starts. This is the monthly release of an egg from an ovary.

Warm-Up

Here are some hormones: testosterone   oestrogen   insulin

Which is the main male reproductive hormone? ....

Which is the main female reproductive hormone? ....

Q1 Tick whether each sentence is true or false.

	True	False
Oestrogen is made in the pituitary gland.	☐	☐
Testosterone stimulates sperm production.	☐	☐
Ovulation is the part of the menstrual cycle when bleeding happens.	☐	☐

Q2 Draw lines to match each hormone with its role in the menstrual cycle.

FSH — helps maintain the uterus lining

LH — causes the release of an egg

progesterone — causes an egg to mature

'Mature' means develop.

NOW TRY THIS

I get round to doing these questions about once a month too...

Hormones cause secondary sexual characteristics to develop at puberty. These are things like facial hair in men and breasts in women.

1) Indah's menstrual cycle lasts 21 days.

   a) Is Indah's menstrual cycle shorter or longer than the average menstrual cycle?

   b) By how many days is Indah's menstrual cycle shorter or longer than the average menstrual cycle?

   c) Indah wants to use a hormonal contraception that she doesn't have to think about taking every day. Suggest one form of contraception that Indah could use.

Topic B5 — Homeostasis and Response

Topic B6 — Inheritance, Variation and Evolution

DNA and Chromosomes

DNA contains all the information you need to build an organism. It's stored in chromosomes.

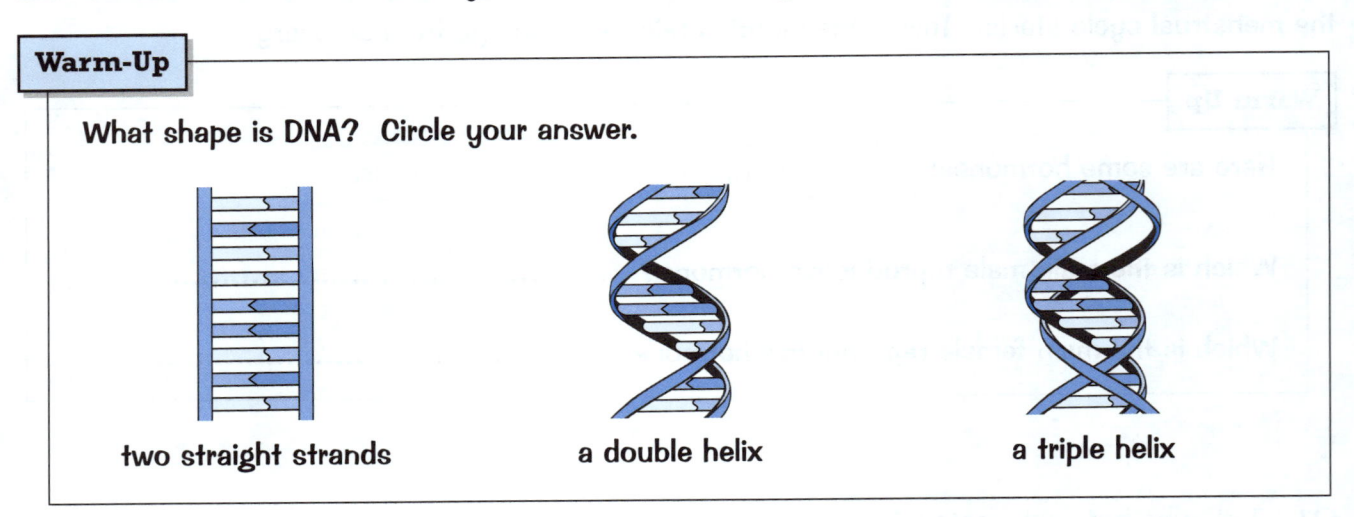

Warm-Up

What shape is DNA? Circle your answer.

- two straight strands
- a double helix
- a triple helix

Q1 What sex chromosomes does a male human have?

☐ XX   ☐ XY   ☐ YY   ☐ XXX

Q2 Add the structures below to the diagram in order of size.

chromosome   gene   genome

....

smallest ⟶ largest

Q3 Choose from the words in boxes to complete the sentences.

Genes are small sections of DNA found on ....

Each gene codes for a particular sequence of ....

These are joined together to make ....

Boxes: amino acids | proteins | chromosomes

Q4 What is a genome?

....

Reproduction

There are two ways of producing offspring — sexual reproduction and asexual reproduction. Asexual reproduction produces identical offspring (clones).

Warm-Up

The pictures show two adult fish and their babies. One of the adult fish produced their babies through asexual reproduction. Which one was this? Circle your answer.

Q1 Which of these cells is a female gamete?

Gametes are sex cells.

☐ sperm cell ☐ skin cell ☐ pollen ☐ egg cell

Q2 Tick a box to complete the sentence.

During sexual reproduction, a male and female gamete...

☐ ...join together at fertilisation. ☐ ...divide to form new cells.

Q3 Circle the words in blue to make these sentences correct.

Meiosis is a type of cell division that happens in sexual / asexual reproduction.

During meiosis, the parent cell divides once / twice . By the end of meiosis,

two / four gametes have been produced. The gametes are identical / non-identical .

NOW TRY THIS

I wonder if horses reproduce using neigh-osis...

Make sure you spend a bit of time learning about meiosis — it can be difficult to get your head around and just as tricky to spell.

1) Giraffes have 30 chromosomes in their normal body cells. They produce offspring through sexual reproduction.

　a) How many chromosomes does a giraffe sperm cell have?

　b) How many chromosomes does a fertilised giraffe egg cell have?

Topic B6 — Inheritance, Variation and Evolution

Genetic Diagrams

I hope you like circles and squares — the next two pages have quite a lot of them.

Warm-Up

An allele is a version of a gene.
How many alleles do you have for each gene in your body? Circle the answer.

1   2   3

Circle the word in blue to complete the sentence.

The mix of alleles you have is called your genotype / chromotype .

Q1 What is a phenotype?

☐ The set of genes an organism has.

☐ The set of chromosomes an organism has.

☐ The set of characteristics an organism has.

Q2 Draw lines to complete the sentences.

| If you have two alleles for a gene that are the same... | ...then you are heterozygous. |
| If you have two alleles for a gene that are different... | ...then you are homozygous. |

Q3 Are the these statements true or false?

	True	False
Red-green colour blindness is caused by a single gene.	☐	☐
Cystic fibrosis is an inherited disorder caused by a dominant allele.	☐	☐
Most characteristics are caused by a single gene.	☐	☐
If you have one recessive allele for a disorder, you will have that disorder.	☐	☐

Topic B6 — Inheritance, Variation and Evolution

Q4 This Punnett square shows how sex is inherited. Fill in the missing X and Y chromosomes.

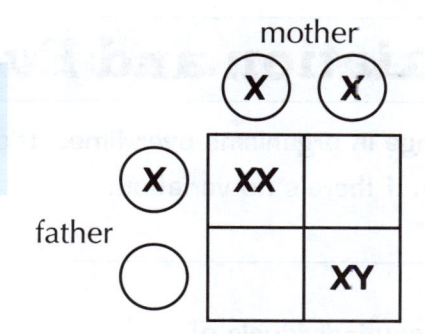

mother

	X	X
X	XX	
		XY

father

Q5 A mouse has a 0.5 chance of inheriting white fur. Circle the diagram that shows this chance as a fraction.

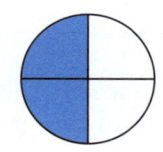

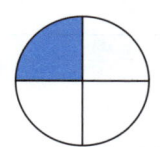

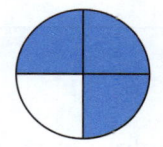

Q6 A Punnett square is shown below. R is a dominant allele. It causes a disorder.

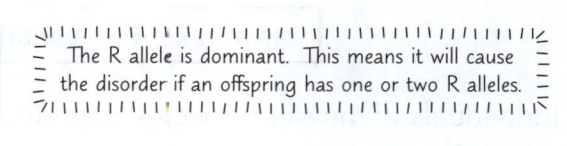

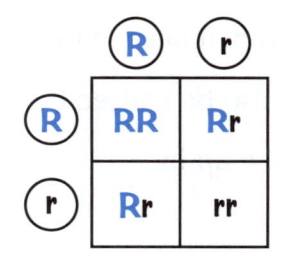

The R allele is dominant. This means it will cause the disorder if an offspring has one or two R alleles.

	R	r
R	RR	Rr
r	Rr	rr

Circle the probability that one of the offspring will have the disorder caused by the R allele.

A person's offspring are their children.

¹/₄   ²/₄   ³/₄

I thought this was a science lesson, not a maths lesson...

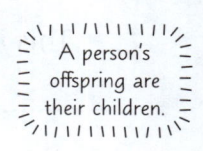

NOW TRY THIS

If you're finding genetic diagrams difficult, the trick is to keep practising. Carry on completing Punnett squares until you're happy you know what you're doing — it's the same each time.

1) A Punnett square for seed colour in a plant species is shown on the right.
   The allele 'G' is dominant. It causes green seeds.
   The allele 'g' is recessive. It causes yellow seeds.

	G	g
G	GG	Gg
g	Gg	gg

   a) The Punnett square shows one offspring with yellow seeds. What alleles does this offspring have?

   b) What is the ratio of green seeds to yellow seeds in the offspring?

   The second Punnett square shows the alleles for different parent plants.

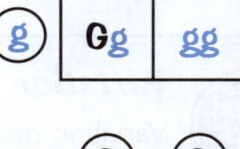

	G	G
G	GG	
g		

   c) Copy this Punnett square and complete it.

   d) What are the possible genotypes of the offspring?

   e) One of the parent plants in this Punnett square is homozygous. What alleles does the homozygous parent plant have?

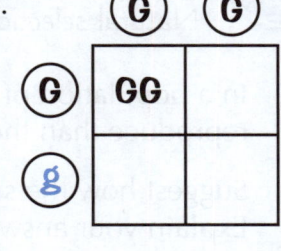

Topic B6 — Inheritance, Variation and Evolution

Variation and Evolution

Evolution is the gradual change in organisms over time. It's a really important idea in biology. And you can't have evolution if there's no variation.

Warm-Up

The table shows how many individuals of three species there are alive in the world.

Which of the species is extinct?

....

Species	Number of individuals
A	6 000 000
B	450
C	0

Q1 Choose from the words below to complete the sentences.

> environment   variation   genes

Individuals of the same species have differences in their characteristics.

This is called .... It may be caused by differences in the

.... inherited from their parents. It may also be caused by

differences in the .... that individuals grew up in.

Q2 Are the these statements true or false?

	True	False
Natural selection prevents evolution from happening.	☐	☐
Life forms first developed around 3 million years ago.	☐	☐
Evolution can lead to new species forming.	☐	☐

NOW TRY THIS

Variation is all around us — just look at my big nose...

Variation means that some individuals are more suited to their environment than others. Natural selection means that these individuals are more likely to survive and reproduce.

1) In a population of deer, males with larger antlers are more likely to survive and reproduce than those with smaller antlers. Antler size is affected by genes.

Suggest how the size of the antlers in this deer population will change over time. Explain your answer.

Topic B6 — Inheritance, Variation and Evolution

Selective Breeding and Genetic Engineering

These two are less complicated than they sound. They both make organisms more useful for us.

Warm-Up

Which of these is a correct description of selective breeding?

☐ Female animals choosing which males to breed with.

☐ Humans choosing which plants or animals are going to breed.

Q1 When did humans first start the selective breeding of plants and animals?

☐ Ten years ago.   ☐ A hundred years ago.   ☐ Thousands of years ago.

Q2 Give one example of an animal that humans have selectively bred.

....

How has this animal changed as a result of selective breeding?

....

Q3 Describe one example of genetic engineering being used to make bacteria more useful to humans.

Genetic engineering involves changing an organism's DNA.

....
....

NOW TRY THIS

I wish I could be genetically engineered to be more useful...

Many crops produce bigger fruits and are resistant to diseases thanks to genetic engineering. This is useful because it means farmers can produce more food.

1) A new disease is destroying snorkel plants.
   There aren't any snorkel plants that are resistant to the disease.

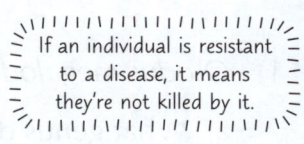

   If an individual is resistant to a disease, it means they're not killed by it.

   a) Zonkfruit trees have a gene that makes them resistant to the disease.
      Outline how genetic engineering could be used to introduce this gene into snorkel plants.

   b) Selective breeding cannot be used to make snorkel plants resistant to the disease.
      Explain why.

Topic B6 — Inheritance, Variation and Evolution

Fossils and Classification

Bit of a mixed bag of stuff here. Fossils are the remains of organisms from millions of years ago. Classification is putting living things into groups, based on how closely related they are.

Warm-Up

What is the name of the classification system that Charles Linnaeus came up with?

☐ Charliean system   ☐ Linnus system   ☐ Linnaean system

Q1 Tick a box to complete the sentence.

Traditionally, organisms were classified in the same group if...

☐ ...they had similar characteristics.   ☐ ...they lived in the same place.

Q2 The classification groups below are shown in order of size, from largest to smallest. Choose from the words in blue to fill in the missing groups.

Genus   Phylum   Order

Kingdom → .... → Class → .... → Family → .... → Species

Q3 Sometimes, an organism does not decay after it dies. Instead it forms a fossil.

Give one reason why an organism might not decay after death.

....

I think that Linnaeus guy had too much time on his hands...

NOW TRY THIS

Fossils can form even when the body is decayed — hard parts of the body, like bones, might be replaced by minerals as they decay. This forms a fossil in the shape of the bones.

1) *Otodus megalodon* is the largest species of shark ever to exist.

   a) What genus does this shark belong to?

   b) What is its species name?

   c) *Otodus megalodon* became extinct over three million years ago. Suggest how we know that it existed.

Topic B6 — Inheritance, Variation and Evolution

Topic B7 — Ecology

Competition and Population Size

Competition isn't just for sports day. Organisms have to compete to survive.

Warm-Up

The sentence in blue is a definition.

The interaction of living organisms with the non-living parts of their environment.

What is it a definition of? ☐ an ecosystem   ☐ a population

Q1 The diagram shows eight factors that can affect population size.

Shade all of the triangles in the diagram that are labelled with biotic factors.

Biotic factors are living factors. Abiotic factors are non-living factors.

(Diagram segments: soil pH, light intensity, temperature, competition, new predators, new pathogens, moisture level, food availability)

Name an abiotic factor not shown in the diagram.

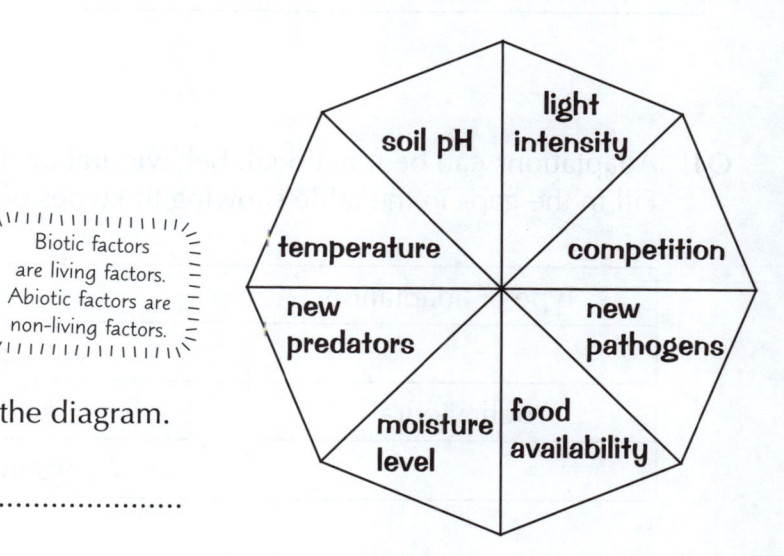

....

Q2 Choose words from the box to fill in the gaps in the paragraph below.

| shelter | depend | change | interdependence |

In a community, different species .... on each other for things like food

and .... This is called .... This means that a big

.... in one part of an ecosystem can affect the whole community.

NOW TRY THIS

I bet you'll finish this question faster than me...

Make sure you've got your head around the stuff on this page. It will make the rest of the topic easier if you have. Promise.

I'm the tallest of them all!

1) Lachlan grows 20 sunflowers in the same flower bed.

   a) Name two things that his sunflowers are competing for.

   The diagram shows part of a food web in Lachlan's flower bed.

   b) If the sunflowers were removed, what might happen to the blue tits?

sunflowers → blue tits → sparrowhawks

Topic B7 — Ecology

Adaptations

If I were adapted to my environment, I'd have an umbrella for a head and wellingtons for feet.

Warm-Up

Circle the words in blue to make these sentences correct.

Organisms are adapted to die / survive in the conditions in their environment.

Adaptations are special features / t-shirts of an organism that suit their environment.

Q1 Adaptations can be functional, behavioural or structural.
Fill in the gaps in the table showing the types of adaptation and their descriptions.

Type of adaptation	Description
	Features of an organism's body structure.
Behavioural	
	Things that go on inside an organism's body.

Q2 Give two features of an environment where an extremophile might live.

Extremophiles are organisms that live in extreme conditions.

1. ....

2. ....

NOW TRY THIS

I adapt really well to being on holiday...

Mountain hares have white fur in the winter, so it's really hard to see them against the snow. This helps them avoid getting eaten by predators. Clever stuff.

1) Camels live in the desert. They have long eyelashes to stop sand blowing into their eyes. They store fat in their hump so that they can survive for a long time without food.

a) Give one structural adaptation found in the camel.

b) Give one functional adaptation found in the camel.

c) The desert is very hot. Camels have a large surface area compared to their volume. Suggest one way that this helps camels to survive in their environment.

Topic B7 — Ecology

Food Chains

Food chains show what gets eaten by what in an ecosystem.

Warm-Up

Which of these is a producer? Circle your answer.

A green plant    My pet rabbit    A box of doughnuts

Q1 Where do producers get energy from to make food?

☐ plants   ☐ the sun   ☐ animals   ☐ energy bars

Q2 Circle the words in blue to make these sentences correct.

Animals that hunt or kill are called **predators / prey**.

The animals that they eat are called **predators / prey**.

Q3 Draw lines to complete the sentences.

Producers are eaten by...	...tertiary consumers.
Primary consumers are eaten by...	...primary consumers.
Secondary consumers are eaten by...	...secondary consumers.

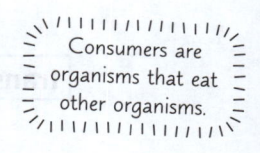

Consumers are organisms that eat other organisms.

NOW TRY THIS

Candy necklaces are my favourite type of food chain...

...spaghetti hoops aren't bad either. When one organism eats another organism, biomass (the mass of living material) is passed along the food chain. Yummy.

1) The diagram shows a food chain.

   grass → grasshopper → shrew → owl

   a) How does the grass make glucose?

   b) Which organism is the secondary consumer?

   c) Which organism is always a predator and never prey?

Topic B7 — Ecology

Using Quadrats and Transects

Time for a trip outside to count some flowers. Only after you've finished these questions though...

Warm-Up

Circle the quadrat.

Q1 Choose from the words to complete the sentence.

distribution | size | lost | found

The .... of an organism is where an organism is ....

Q2 Draw lines to match each sampling method with the correct description.

quadrats — Used to study the distribution of plants along a line.

transects — Used to randomly sample plants in a field.

Q3 The sentences below describe using a quadrat to see how common an organism is in a sample area. Number the boxes to put them in the correct order. The first one has been done for you.

☐ Count all the organisms you're interested in within the quadrat.

[1] Place a quadrat on the ground in the sample area.

☐ Work out the mean number of organisms per quadrat within the sample area.

☐ Place the quadrat in another part of the sample area and count the organisms.

Topic B7 — Ecology

Q4 Two students want to find out if daisies become more or less common as you move from a hedge towards the middle of a field. They are trying to decide what method to use. Which student is correct? Circle their name.

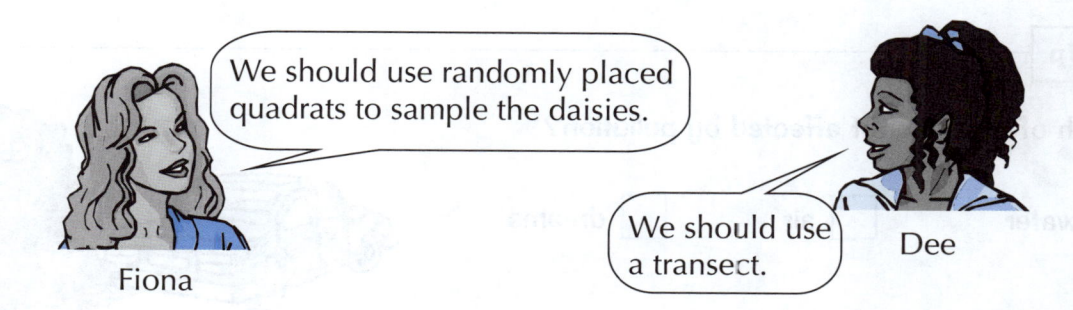

Fiona: We should use randomly placed quadrats to sample the daisies.

Dee: We should use a transect.

Q5 Give two ways that you can collect data along a transect.

1. ....

2. ....

Q6 Sanjeep counted a total of 75 buttercups in 5 quadrats in a sample area.

Which calculation would Sanjeep need to do to calculate the mean number of buttercups per quadrat?

☐ mean = $\frac{75}{5}$ ☐ mean = $\frac{5}{75}$ ☐ mean = 5 × 75

Calculate the mean number of buttercups per quadrat.

Mean = ... buttercups per quadrat

NOW TRY THIS

Stop and smell the roses — if you're a biologist count them too...

Quadrats and transects don't tell you why there is more or less of an organism in a particular place. You have to think about the environment to work this out.

1) Sandra uses a quadrat to sample poppies in a field.

   a) She recorded the following results: 14, 16, 18, 20.
   What is the total number of poppies?

   b) Calculate the mean number of poppies per quadrat.

   c) The quadrat has an area of 0.25 m². The field has an area of 600 m². How many times does the quadrat fit into the field?

   d) Estimate the population of poppies in the field.

Topic B7 — Ecology

Biodiversity and Human Activity

Biodiversity is the variety of different species of organisms on Earth, or within an ecosystem. Human activity can cause all sorts of problems for biodiversity. Boo.

Warm-Up

Which of these is not affected by pollution?

☐ water   ☐ air   ☐ dreams

Which of these pollutes land?

☐ smoke   ☐ acidic gases   ☐ household waste

Q1 Tick whether each sentence is true or false.

	True	False
The human population has stopped growing.	☐	☐
Increasing the standard of living means more resources are used.	☐	☐
If waste is not handled properly it can cause pollution.	☐	☐
Carbon dioxide is the only greenhouse gas.	☐	☐

Q2 Choose words from the box to fill in the gaps in the paragraph below.

> measures   survive   maintained   reducing

For the human species to ...., it's important that a good level of biodiversity is .... Lots of human actions are .... biodiversity. It's only recently that we've started taking .... to stop biodiversity decreasing.

Q3 Give one way that pollution reduces biodiversity.

....

Topic B7 — Ecology

Q4 Fill in the crossword using the clues. Some letters have been filled in for you.

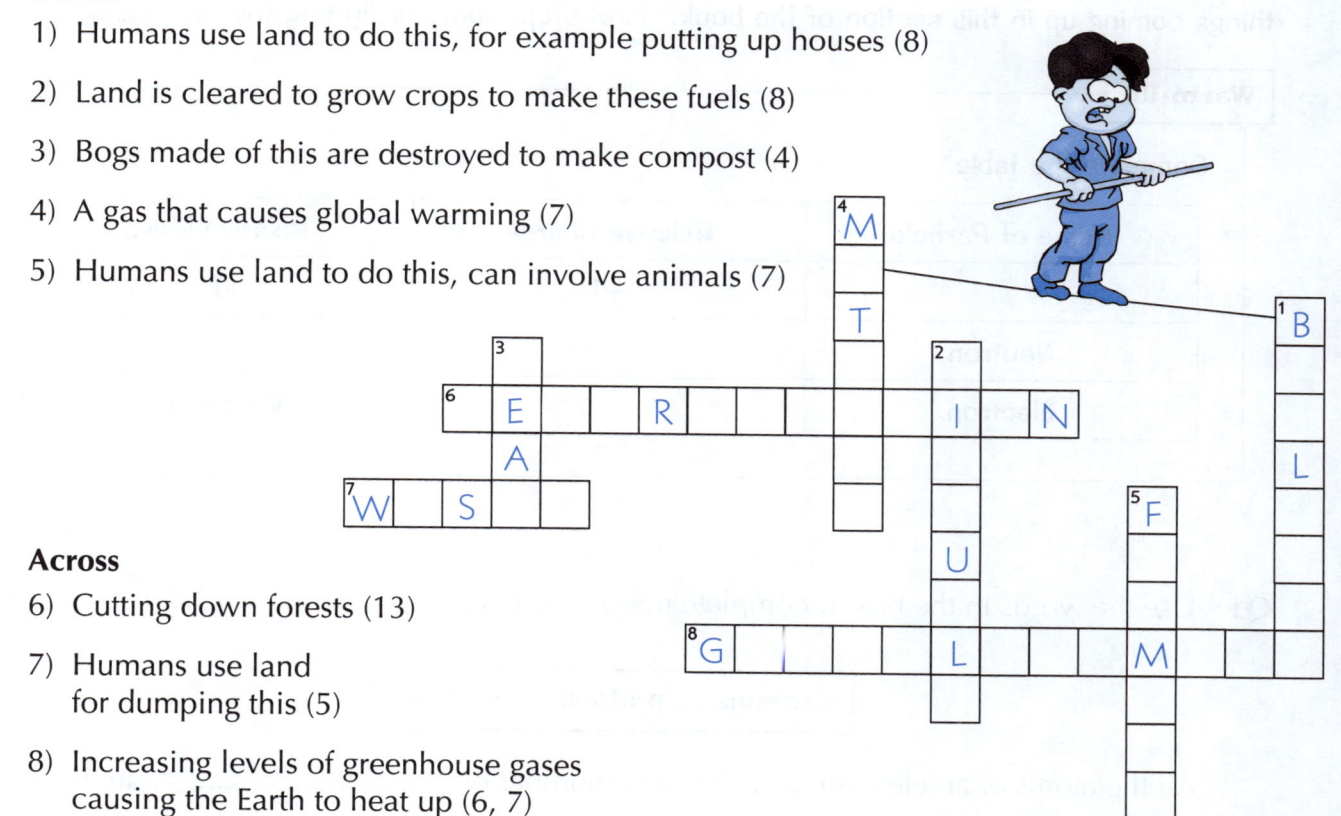

Down
1) Humans use land to do this, for example putting up houses (8)
2) Land is cleared to grow crops to make these fuels (8)
3) Bogs made of this are destroyed to make compost (4)
4) A gas that causes global warming (7)
5) Humans use land to do this, can involve animals (7)

Across
6) Cutting down forests (13)
7) Humans use land for dumping this (5)
8) Increasing levels of greenhouse gases causing the Earth to heat up (6, 7)

Try all these questions — don't let any go to waste...

NOW TRY THIS Having a high biodiversity is a good thing — it can make an ecosystem more stable. This means that everything is nicely in balance. Happy days.

1) The bar chart shows the number of species of birds found in three gardens.

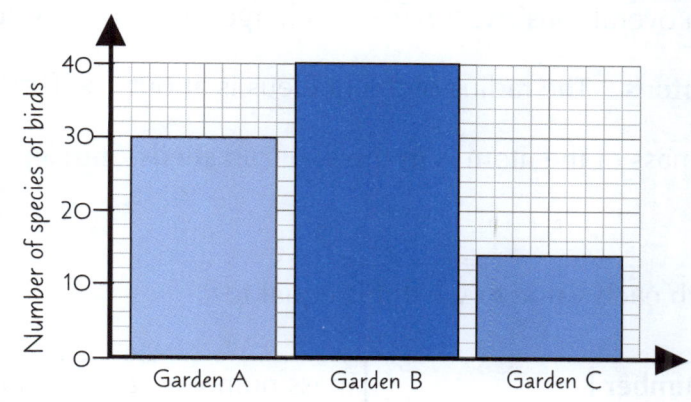

   a) How many species of birds does Garden B have?

   b) How many more species of birds does Garden B have than Garden C?

   c) Which garden has the highest bird biodiversity?

   d) How might a higher bird biodiversity make the ecosystem in a garden more stable?

Topic B7 — Ecology

Topic C1 — Atomic Structure and the Periodic Table

Atoms and Elements

Welcome to the world of chemistry. You're in for a treat — there's a whole load of really exciting things coming up in this section of the book. First stop, some really tiny things. Really, really tiny.

Warm-Up

Complete the table.

Name of Particle	Relative Charge	Relative Mass
	+1	1
Neutron		
Electron		Very small

Q1 Use the words in the box to complete these sentences.

electrons   protons   neutrons

All the atoms of an element have the same number of .... in the nucleus.

Isotopes are atoms of the same element that have different numbers of ....

Atoms always have an equal number of protons and ....

Q2 Circle the words in blue to make these sentences about the nucleus of an atom correct.

The nucleus has an overall **positive / negative** charge. The nucleus contains neutrons and **electrons / protons**. The radius of the nucleus is about 1×10^{-14} **miles / metres**. Almost the whole mass of the atom is in the **electron shells / nucleus**.

Q3 Draw lines to match each value to what it is equal to.

atomic number   mass number – atomic number

mass number   number of protons

number of neutrons   number of protons + number of neutrons

Q4 Tick whether each statement about atoms is true or false.

	True	False
The smallest amount of an element you can have is one atom of that element.	☐	☐
An atom has a radius of about 0.1 nanometres.	☐	☐
Atoms have an overall positive charge.	☐	☐
There are about 1000 different elements shown on the periodic table.	☐	☐

Q5 Boron has two stable isotopes.
The abundance of B-10 is 20% and the abundance of B-11 is 80%.
Use the formula to write the correct value in each box below, then complete the calculation to find the relative atomic mass of boron to 1 decimal place.

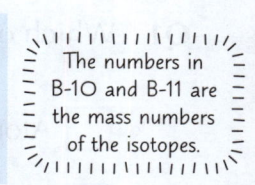

The numbers in B-10 and B-11 are the mass numbers of the isotopes.

$$\text{Relative atomic mass } (A_r) \text{ of boron} = \frac{\left(\substack{\text{abundance} \\ \text{of B-10}} \times \substack{\text{mass number} \\ \text{of B-10}}\right) + \left(\substack{\text{abundance} \\ \text{of B-11}} \times \substack{\text{mass number} \\ \text{of B-11}}\right)}{\text{abundance of B-10} + \text{abundance of B-11}}$$

$$A_r \text{ of boron} = \frac{(\boxed{} \times \boxed{}) + (\boxed{} \times \boxed{})}{\boxed{} + \boxed{}}$$

A_r of boron = ...

Don't trust atoms — they make up everything...

NOW TRY THIS

There's more on elements coming up later in this topic, so it's important you know what all the different numbers mean. This question should check that you understand what's going on.

1) The nuclear symbol for thorium is shown on the right.

   a) How many protons does a thorium atom have?

   b) How many neutrons does a thorium atom have?

   $^{232}_{90}\text{Th}$

   Thorium ions have a 4+ charge.

   c) How many electrons does a thorium 4+ ion have?

Topic C1 — Atomic Structure and the Periodic Table

Compounds and Equations

Hold up — it's not just atoms and elements you've got to get your head around. Combine a bunch of different ones and you've got a whole load of compounds to know about too. How exciting.

Warm-Up

Circle the words in black to make these sentences correct.

During a chemical reaction, at least one new **atom / substance** is made.

Often, a change in **energy / weather** can be measured.

Q1 Which of these statements about compounds is true?

☐ Atoms in a compound are held together by glue.

☐ Any substance that contains two or more atoms is a compound.

☐ Compounds are substances that contain atoms of two or more elements.

☐ Two molecules of water could have different numbers of atoms in them.

Q2 How many atoms are in one molecule of H_2SO_4?

☐ 3   ☐ 5   ☐ 6   ☐ 7

Q3 Sort the substances below into the right columns in the table.

Elements	Compounds

HCl P_4 CO_2 H_2O O_2 S_8 NH_3 C_{60}

Topic C1 — Atomic Structure and the Periodic Table

Q4 Use the words in the box to complete these sentences.

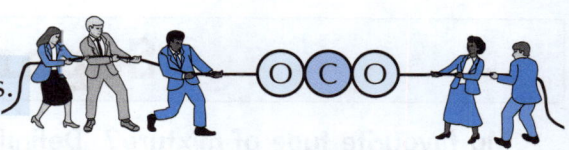

| reaction | elements | bonds | sieve |

Compounds are held together by chemical .... The only way to separate a compound into its .... is by using a chemical ....

Q5 The equation below shows how plants make food from carbon dioxide and water.

Write down how many atoms of each type are on each side.

$$6CO_2 + 6H_2O \rightarrow C_6H_{12}O_6 + 5O_2$$

Reactants: C atoms ....   Products: C atoms ....

H atoms ....   H atoms ....

O atoms ....   O atoms ....

Is this equation balanced?   **Yes / No**

Q6 Sodium reacts with oxygen to make sodium oxide. Balance the symbol equation for this reaction.

.... Na + O$_2$ → .... Na$_2$O

Revision + Practice → Success...

NOW TRY THIS

Equations don't have to be complicated — think carefully about which things are the reactants and which are the products. Put them on the correct sides and Bob's your uncle.

1) Levi reacts magnesium hydroxide with hydrochloric acid to make magnesium chloride and water.

   a) Write a word equation for this reaction.

   Magnesium chloride contains one atom of magnesium (Mg) for every two atoms of chlorine (Cl).

   b) Write the formula for magnesium chloride.

   c) Complete the balanced equation for the reaction, using the answer to b).

   Mg(OH)$_2$ + ... HCl → .... + ... H$_2$O

Topic C1 — Atomic Structure and the Periodic Table

Separating Mixtures

My favourite type of mixture? Definitely cake. I promise these separation methods are easier to learn than trying to get an egg back out of some brownie batter. Better get cracking.

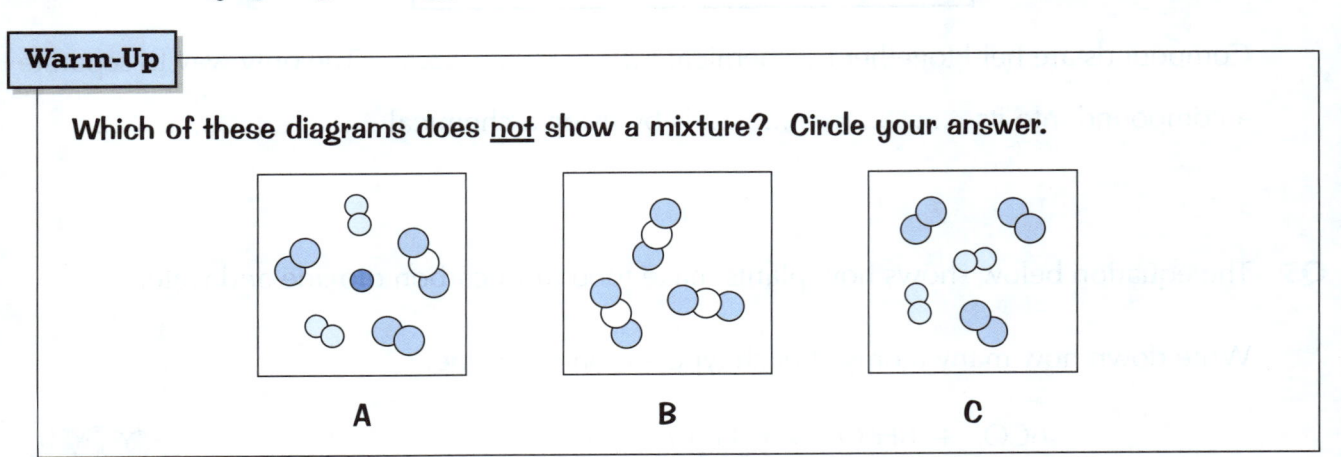

Warm-Up

Which of these diagrams does not show a mixture? Circle your answer.

A   B   C

Q1 Tick whether each statement below is true or false.

	True	False
There are chemical bonds between the different parts of a mixture.	☐	☐
Different parts of a mixture can be separated using physical methods.	☐	☐
A substance in a mixture keeps its own chemical properties.	☐	☐
Physical separation methods form new substances.	☐	☐

Q2 Draw lines to match each separation technique to its purpose.

fractional distillation — separates insoluble solids from liquids

crystallisation — separates soluble solids from solutions

filtration — separates a mixture of liquids

Q3 Which one of these properties allows liquids to be separated using fractional distillation?

☐ colour   ☐ melting point   ☐ boiling point   ☐ tastiness

Topic C1 — Atomic Structure and the Periodic Table

Q4 The steps below are from a chromatography experiment to separate the dyes in an ink. Number the steps in the correct order. The first one has been done for you.

.... When the solvent has nearly reached the top of the paper, take the paper out.

.... Pour a small amount of solvent into a beaker and place the sheet of paper in it.

...**1**.... Draw a line near the bottom of a sheet of filter paper in pencil.

.... Place a lid on top of the beaker.

.... Add a spot of ink to the line.

crow-photography

Q5 The apparatus used for fractional distillation is shown below.

Draw lines between the labels and the correct letters on the diagram.

Hottest bit of the column

Coolest bit of the column

What is the condenser for?

....

....

All these separation methods have made a right mixture in my head...

NOW TRY THIS

An artist once filled an abandoned, waterproofed apartment with 75 000 litres of copper sulfate solution to make a whole apartment filled with crystals. True story, look it up.

1) Jessie is trying to make some copper sulfate crystals.
   She has a solution of copper sulfate.

   a) Why can she not use filtration to get copper sulfate crystals from the solution?

   Jessie decides to use crystallisation to make crystals from her solution.

   b) Describe how she could use crystallisation to make copper sulfate crystals from her solution.

Topic C1 — Atomic Structure and the Periodic Table

Electronic Structure and the Periodic Table

Back to those electrons and elements now. You need to know about how the electrons in elements are arranged. Electronic structures will help you understand the patterns in the periodic table.

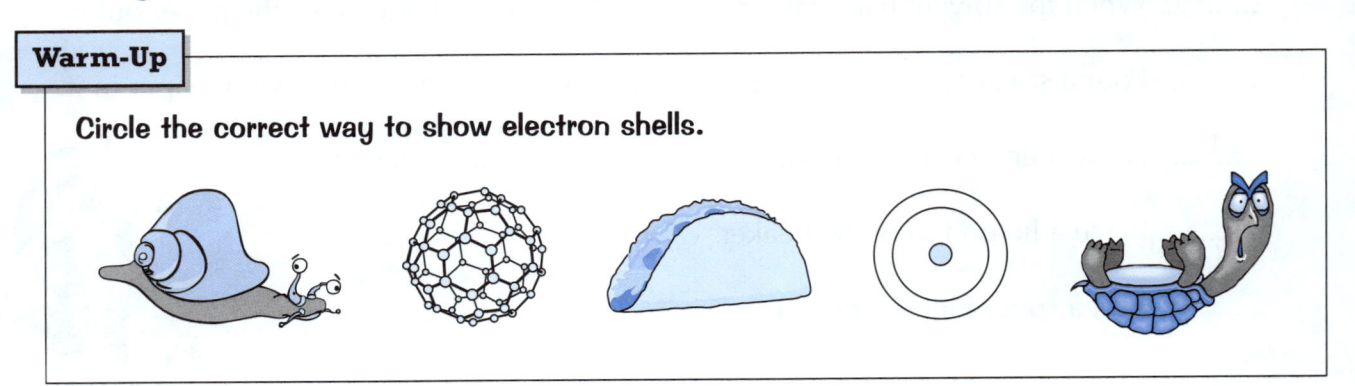

Warm-Up

Circle the correct way to show electron shells.

Q1 Circle the words in blue to make these sentences correct.

The periodic table is laid out in order of increasing **atomic / mass** number.

It gets its name from the **random / repeating** patterns in element properties.

Elements in the same **column / row** have similar properties.

Q2 Use the words in the box to complete these sentences.

| inner | energy levels | full | outer | rings | empty |

Electrons move in shells — these are sometimes called ....

The .... shells fill up first. These are the ones closest to the nucleus.

Atoms are most stable when they have .... electron shells.

Q3 Oxygen has the electronic structure 2, 6.
Complete the electronic structure diagram for oxygen.

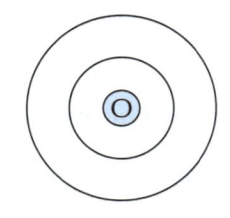

Topic C1 — Atomic Structure and the Periodic Table

Q4 The atomic number of sodium is 11.
What is the electronic structure of sodium?

.........., ..., ...

Q5 The electronic structures for four different elements are shown below.
Tick the element (or elements) that correctly answer each question.

Be   Ne   H   Mg

	Be	Ne	H	Mg
Which of these elements is the most stable?	☐	☐	☐	☐
Which two of these elements have two full electron shells?	☐	☐	☐	☐
Which two of these elements are in the same group?	☐	☐	☐	☐
Which element needs one extra electron to fill its outer shell?	☐	☐	☐	☐

CGP chemistry jokes get updated periodically...

NOW TRY THIS
Electronic structures can be easy as long as you know the rules. Only a certain number of electrons are allowed in each shell — 2 in the first, and 8 in the second and third.

1) Eilidh has drawn the electronic structure of sulfur (atomic number = 16).

   a) What is wrong with her electronic structure?

   b) Write the correct electronic structure of sulfur in number form.

   c) Draw the correct electronic structure of sulfur.

   Oxygen is above sulfur in the periodic table.
   Chlorine is to the right of sulfur in the periodic table.

   d) Will the properties of sulfur be more similar to the properties of oxygen or to the properties of chlorine? Explain your answer.

Topic C1 — Atomic Structure and the Periodic Table

Metals and Non-Metals

It's time to take a look at the arrangement of elements in the periodic table. You need to know how they're divided into metals and non-metals — thankfully they're grouped together pretty nicely.

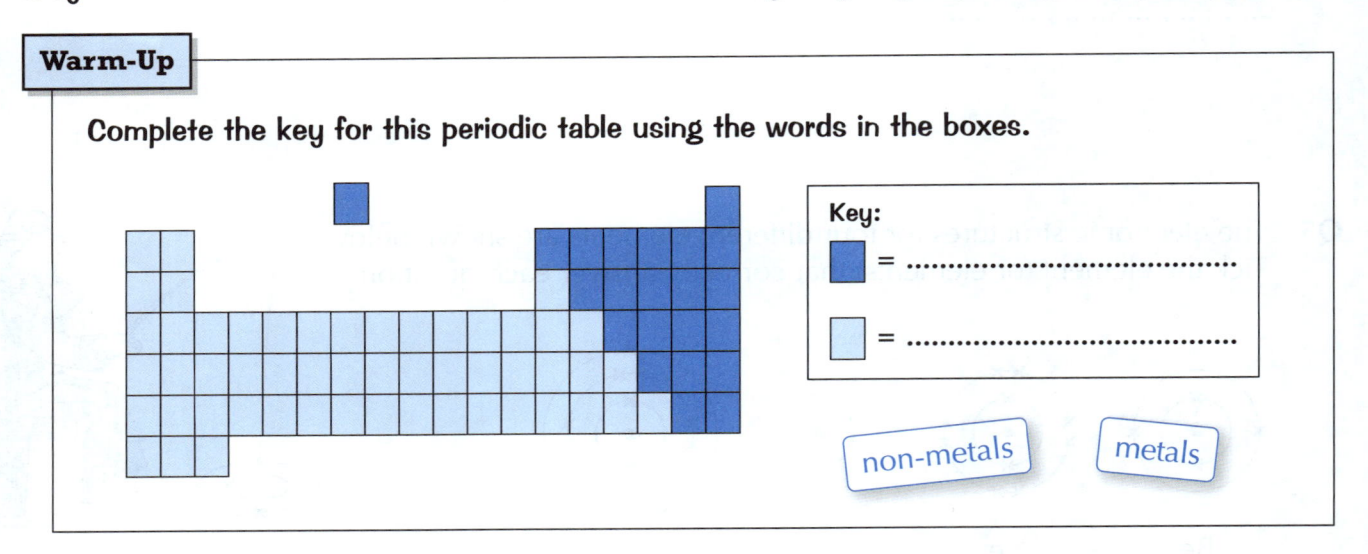

Warm-Up

Complete the key for this periodic table using the words in the boxes.

Key:
■ = ...
□ = ...

non-metals   metals

Q1 Metals and non-metals have different physical properties.
Tick whether the statements below are true for metals or non-metals.

	metals	non-metals
These are great at conducting heat and electricity.	☐	☐
These tend to be brittle (they can break easily if you bend them).	☐	☐
These often have a low density.	☐	☐
These usually have high melting and boiling points.	☐	☐
These usually form positive ions when they react.	☐	☐
These are malleable (can be bent or hammered into different shapes).	☐	☐

Call a copper — these metal puns are really getting old...

NOW TRY THIS

That staircase-like line on the periodic table will be your best friend sooner or later. It's super handy for figuring out the properties of an unknown element based on its position.

1) Amy has facts about four unknown elements. These facts are shown in the table on the right. Amy knows two of the elements are metals and two are non-metals.

Which of the elements are more likely to be the metals? Which are more likely to be the non-metals?

Element	Fact
A	boiling point: −188 °C
B	poor conductor of heat
C	boiling point: 3287 °C
D	excellent electrical conductor

Topic C1 — Atomic Structure and the Periodic Table

Group 1

Alkali metals are quite different to what I think of as a metal — they're soft rather than hard, and they're also flippin' reactive. Like an angry koala, I suppose. Cuddly, but not to be messed with.

Warm-Up

In Group 1, reactivity increases as you go down the group.
For each pair of alkali metals, circle the metal that is most reactive.

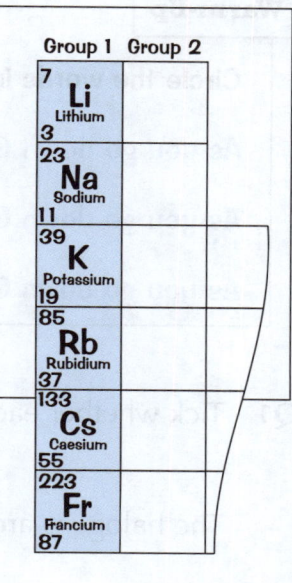

francium   or   potassium

sodium   or   rubidium

lithium   or   caesium

Group 1	Group 2
7 Li Lithium 3	
23 Na Sodium 11	
39 K Potassium 19	
85 Rb Rubidium 37	
133 Cs Caesium 55	
223 Fr Francium 87	

Q1 How many electrons are in the outer shell of Group 1 elements?

☐ 1   ☐ 2   ☐ 4   ☐ 7

Q2 Alkali metals react with chlorine to make metal chlorides.
Write a word equation for the reaction between sodium and chlorine.

.... + ... → ....

Q3 Alkali metals react with oxygen to make metal oxides.
Balance the symbol equation for the reaction of potassium with oxygen.

.... K + O$_2$ → .... K$_2$O

Want to hear a joke about sodium? Na...

NOW TRY THIS

I wouldn't recommend cuddling an alkali metal — their reactions can be pretty vigorous. Make sure you can describe what happens in reactions with oxygen, chlorine and water.

1) Zebulun is investigating the reactivity of potassium and lithium with water.
   Alkali metals react with water to produce a metal hydroxide and hydrogen.

   a) Write a word equation for the reaction between lithium and water.

   b) Describe what Zebulun would see for the reactions
      of potassium and lithium with water.

Topic C1 — Atomic Structure and the Periodic Table

Group 7

Like the rest of the periodic table, there are patterns in the halogens in Group 7.
It's all to do with the fact they have the same number of outer shell electrons again.

Warm-Up

Circle the words in black to make these sentences correct.

As you go down Group 7, the halogens have **higher / lower** melting and boiling points.

As you go down Group 7, the relative atomic masses **increase / decrease**.

As you go down Group 7, the halogens become **more / less** reactive.

Q1 Tick whether each statement about the halogens is true or false.

	True	False
The halogens are metals.	☐	☐
The halogens all have 7 electrons in their outer shell.	☐	☐
Two halogen atoms join together to form a molecule of the element.	☐	☐

Q2 Use the words in the box to complete these sentences.

| ionic | covalent | metal | non-metals | halides |

Halogens form ions called .... These form ionic bonds
with .... ions to make compounds with .... structures.

Halogen atoms react with non-metals to form .... bonds.

NOW TRY THIS

I'm the most horrible of my friends — I'm the bro-mean...

It's crazy how something as poisonous as chlorine can make something as common as the salt we put on our food (sodium chloride). I suppose that's chemistry for you — full of surprises.

1) Talitha is carrying out halogen displacement reactions with bromine.
   She adds bromine to a solution of sodium iodide. A reaction takes place.

   a) Explain why a reaction takes place.

   b) Write a word equation for the reaction.

   She then adds bromine to a solution of sodium chloride.

   c) Will a reaction take place? Explain your answer.

Topic C1 — Atomic Structure and the Periodic Table

Group 0

And now, the fanciest of all the elements, the noble gases. They're all colourless, don't really react with anything, but they can make funky coloured lights. Buckle up, it's going to be a wild ride.

Warm-Up

Which of these is a noble gas? Circle your answer.

boron   radon   aluminium   Duchess Tonya

silicon   oxygen   selenium

Q1 All but one of the noble gases have eight outer shell electrons. Which noble gas only has two outer shell electrons?

☐ argon   ☐ helium   ☐ krypton   ☐ neon

Q2 Which of these statements about the noble gases is true?

☐ As you go down Group 0, the relative atomic masses of the elements decrease.

☐ As you go down Group 0, the boiling points of the elements increase.

Q3 Use electron shells to explain why noble gas elements exist as single atoms.

....

....

Which elements invented the door knocker? The no-bell gases...

NOW TRY THIS — This question is about one of the patterns in the periodic table — you need to be able predict how the properties of noble gases change as you go up or down Group 0.

Group 0: He Helium, Ne Neon, Ar Argon, Kr Krypton, Xe Xenon

1) Argon is a gas at 0 °C.

   a) Predict the state of neon at 0 °C.

   Argon has a boiling point of –186 °C. Xenon has a boiling point of –108 °C.

   b) Which of these is most likely to be the boiling point of krypton?

   ☐ –103 °C   ☐ –153 °C   ☐ –203 °C

Topic C1 — Atomic Structure and the Periodic Table

Ionic Bonding

Bonding and structure sound pretty tricky, but they don't need to be. There are three different types of bonding to learn, and they're all to do with electrons. Bish bash bosh.

Warm-Up

Use the numbers on the right to complete these sentences about elements.

Most Group .... and Group .... elements are non-metals.

All Group .... and Group .... elements are metals.

| 1 | 2 | 6 | 7 |

Q1 Use the words in the box to complete the sentences about ions.

| negative   charged   equal to   positive   greater than |

Ions are .... particles formed when atoms gain or lose electrons.

Metal atoms lose electrons from their outer shell to form .... ions.

Non-metal atoms gain electrons into their outer shell to form .... ions.

The number of electrons lost or gained is .... the charge on the ion.

Q2 Are the statements below true or false?

True   False

Some atoms will lose electrons to get a full outer shell. ☐ ☐

An ion with a full outer shell has the same electronic structure as a noble gas. ☐ ☐

A full outer shell is not very stable. ☐ ☐

Q3 Match each group to the charge on the ions formed by its elements.

Group 1   1−

Group 2   2+

Group 6   1+

Group 7   2−

Topic C2 — Bonding, Structure and Properties of Matter

Q4 Circle the words in blue to make these sentences correct.

There are **magnetic / electrostatic** forces of attraction between oppositely charged ions.

This attraction is called an ionic bond — it holds metal ions and non-metal ions together to make an ionic **compound / collection**.

Lots of ions can be held together to form a **small / giant** structure.

The forces of attraction act in **most / all** directions.

Q5 Sodium chloride is made from sodium and chlorine ions. Sodium is a group 1 metal, and chlorine is a group 7 non-metal. A sodium atom and a chlorine atom are shown on the right. Complete the dot and cross diagram for sodium chloride.

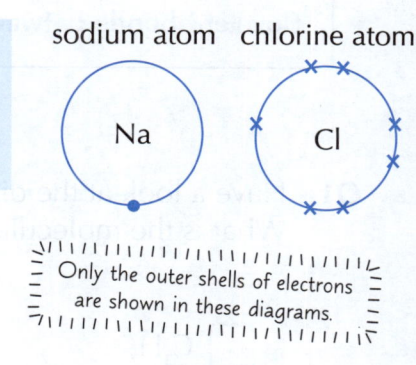

Only the outer shells of electrons are shown in these diagrams.

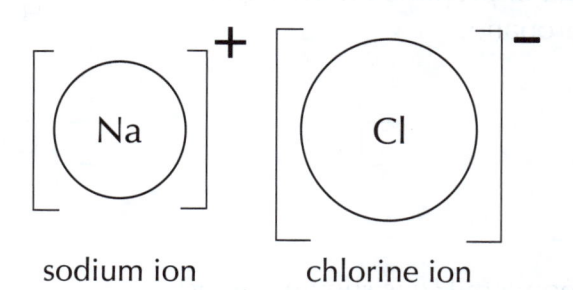

Q6 Draw a dot and cross diagram to show how lithium (a Group 1 metal) and oxygen (a Group 6 non-metal) form lithium oxide (Li_2O). Include arrows to show the movement of electrons.

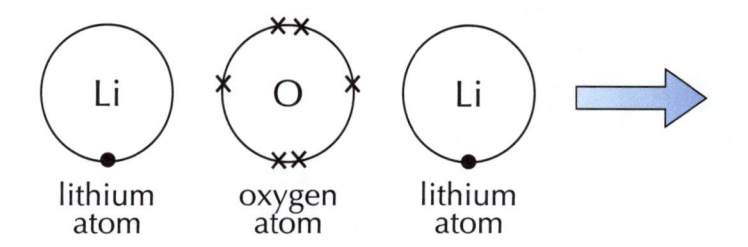

"Are you sure you've lost electrons?" "I'm positive..."

Remember, those negative ions have taken one (or more) electrons for the team so that ions can bond together. It's all about the attraction between oppositely charged ions, after all.

1) Use the dot and cross diagram for strontium bromide ($SrBr_2$) to answer these questions:

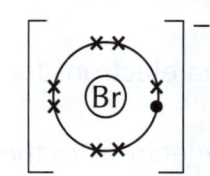

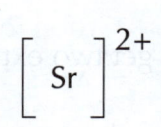

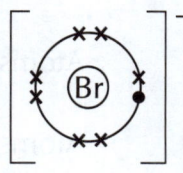

   a) Which of the ions is a metal?

   b) What is the group number of bromine? How can you tell from the diagram?

   c) How many electrons are in the outer shell of a strontium atom? Explain how you know.

Topic C2 — Bonding, Structure and Properties of Matter

Covalent Bonding

Oh good, another type of bonding to get your head around. This one's all about sharing electrons. We could all learn a thing or two from covalent bonds. Sharing is caring, after all.

Warm-Up

Circle the words in black to make these sentences correct.

Covalent bonds are formed when **non-metals / metals** bond together.

Covalent bonds are formed when atoms **swap / share** pairs of electrons.

Covalent bonds between atoms are very **weak / strong**.

Q1 Have a look at the displayed formula of propane on the right. What is the molecular formula of propane?

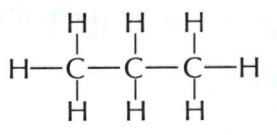

☐ C_3H_7 ☐ C_2H_8 ☐ C_3H_8 ☐ C_3H_6

Q2 The dot and cross diagram for ammonia (NH_3) is shown below. Draw the displayed formula of ammonia in the space below.

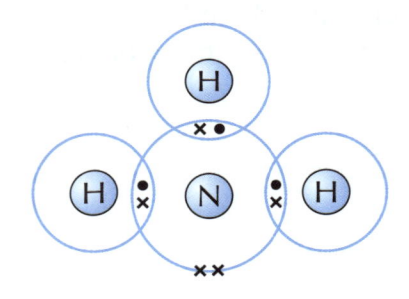

Q3 The statements below are about covalent bonding. Decide whether each one is true or false.

	True	False
Atoms make enough covalent bonds to fill up their outer shells.	☐	☐
Atoms get two extra electrons for each single covalent bond they form.	☐	☐
Atoms only share electrons in their outer shells.	☐	☐

Topic C2 — Bonding, Structure and Properties of Matter

Q4 In a displayed formula, what does each line show?

....

Q5 Complete the dot and cross diagram for water (H₂O) below.

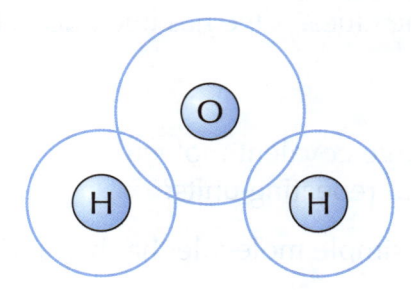

Q6 The displayed formula for methane (CH₄) is shown. Draw a dot and cross diagram for methane in the space below.

H
|
H—C—H
|
H

Q7 Dot and cross diagrams for oxygen (O₂) and nitrogen (N₂) are shown below. Describe one difference in the bonding in these molecules.

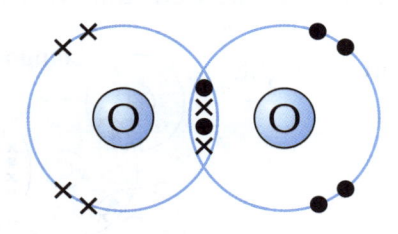

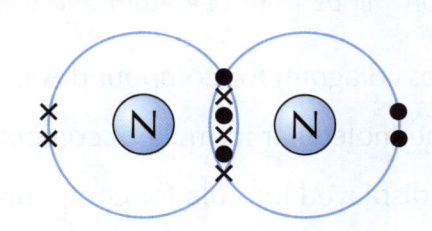

....

....

Topic C2 — Bonding, Structure and Properties of Matter

Q8 Polymers are examples of very large covalent molecules. A diagram of a polymer called poly(ethene) is shown on the right.

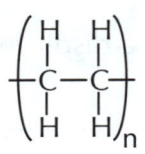

What does the little 'n' outside of the brackets mean?

....

Q9 Fill in the crossword using the clues. One has been done for you.

Across

2) What name is given to large covalent molecules that are made up of lots of repeating units?

5) What is an example of a simple molecule that has a triple bond?

6) What molecule is made from one H atom and one Cl atom?

8) What substance has the molecular formula NH_3?

9) What type of covalent bond is found in oxygen, O_2?

Down

1) What is an example of a giant covalent structure that is made up of silicon and oxygen?

3) How many covalent bonds are there in methane, CH_4?

4) A covalent bond is formed when two atoms .... a pair of electrons.

7) What is an example of a giant covalent structure that is made from carbon?*

*Hint: it makes nice jewellery...

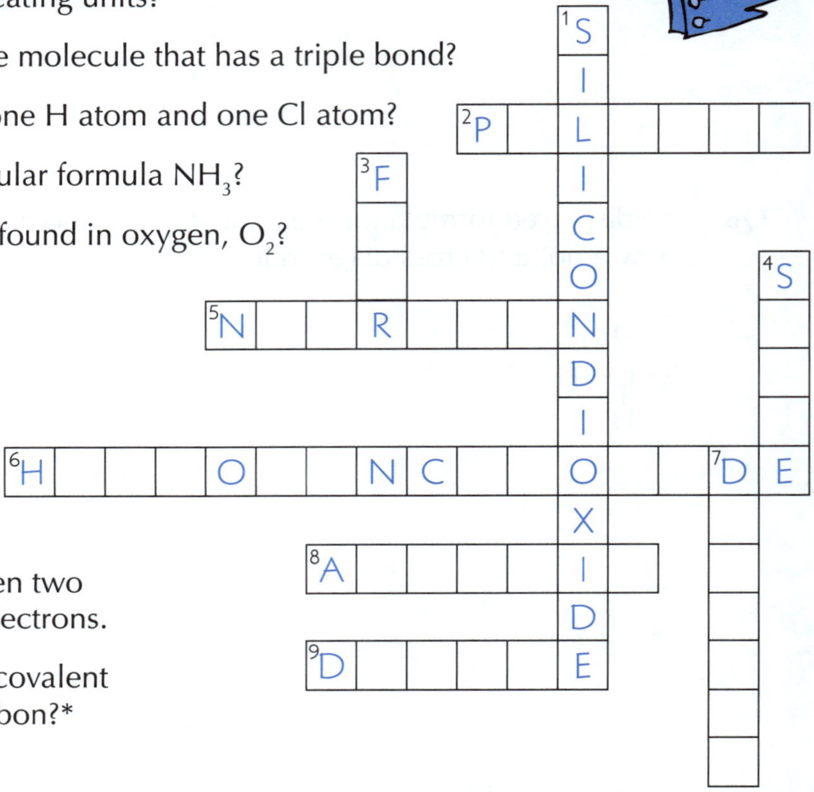

Dot your electrons and cross your, well, electrons...

NOW TRY THIS Don't forget, when you're drawing a single covalent bond on a dot and cross diagram, one electron will be from one atom and the other electron will be from the other atom.

1) A dot and cross diagram for compound A is shown on the right.

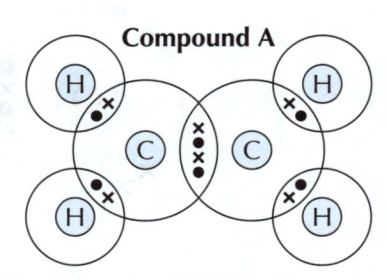

   a) What is the molecular formula of compound A?

   b) Draw the displayed formula for compound A.

   Compound A reacts with chlorine (Cl_2) to make compound B.

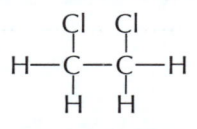

   c) What is the molecular formula of compound B?

   d) How many covalent bonds are in compound B?

Topic C2 — Bonding, Structure and Properties of Matter

Metallic Bonding

Time for some bonding in metals. Just to make it clear, metallic bonding is not the love story between some tin foil and an aluminium can. It is, in fact, about electrons.

Warm-Up

Metallic bonding happens in metals and alloys. Which two of these are alloys?

☐ A mixture of two or more non-metals.   ☐ A mixture of two or more metals.

☐ A mixture of a metal and another element.

Q1 Circle the words in blue to make these sentences correct.

Metals are **small / giant** structures of atoms. They contain lots of metal atoms bonded together in a **random / regular** pattern. The electrons in the **outer / inner** shell of the metal atoms are delocalised — they are free to move. There are strong forces of attraction between the **positive / negative** metal ions and the shared **positive / negative** electrons.

Q2 The diagram below shows metallic bonding. Add labels to the diagram.

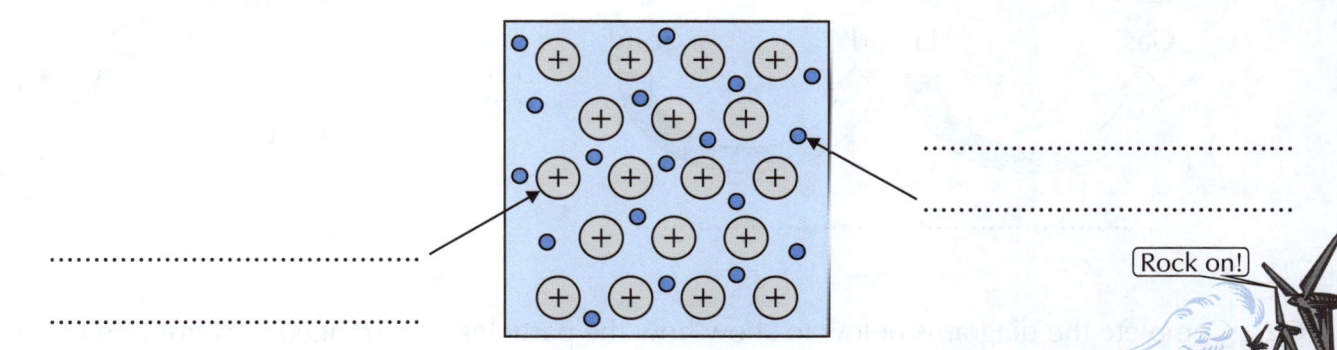

What music do wind turbines like? They're huge metal fans...

NOW TRY THIS This last question is a little challenging, but don't be put off. Think carefully about the structure of metals and alloys and you'll do just fine.

Use the periodic table at the back of the book to help you.

1) The table shows the composition of three materials.

   a) Which of the materials are alloys?

   Materials conduct electricity when a charged particle is able to move through the structure and carry the charge.

   b) Suggest why material B can conduct electricity.

Material	Composition
A	97% Fe, 3% C
B	65% Cu, 35% Zn
C	82% N, 18% H

Topic C2 — Bonding, Structure and Properties of Matter

States of Matter

Just like that, we've reached the final pages of this topic. What a journey. Don't celebrate just yet though — have a go at these questions on states of matter and changes of state first.

Warm-Up

Circle any things that are solid at room temperature.

oxygen, screw, milk, wood, water, pencil, paperclip, air

Q1 Use the words on the right to label the changes of state.

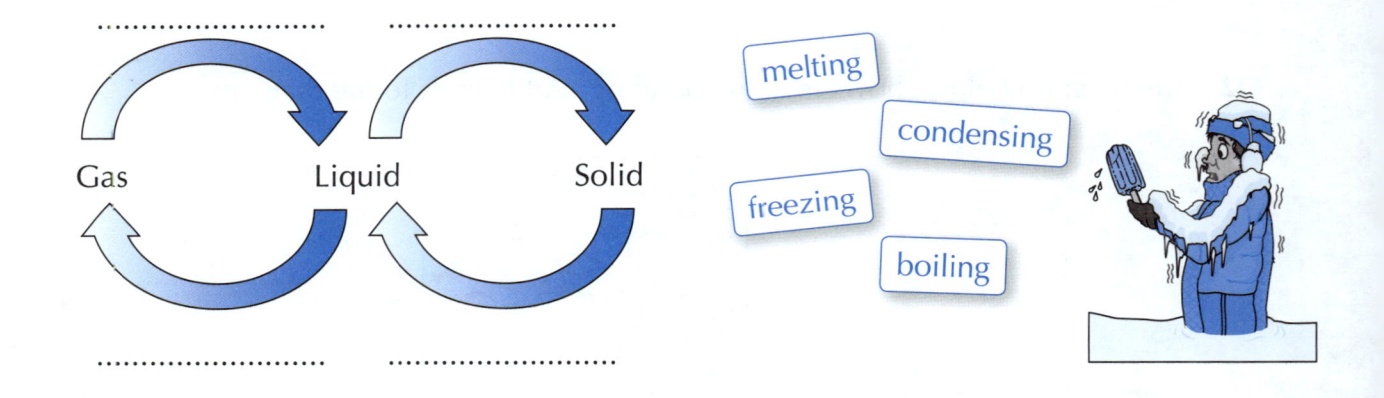

Gas → Liquid → Solid

melting, condensing, freezing, boiling

Q2 Complete the diagrams below to show how the particles are arranged in solids and gases.

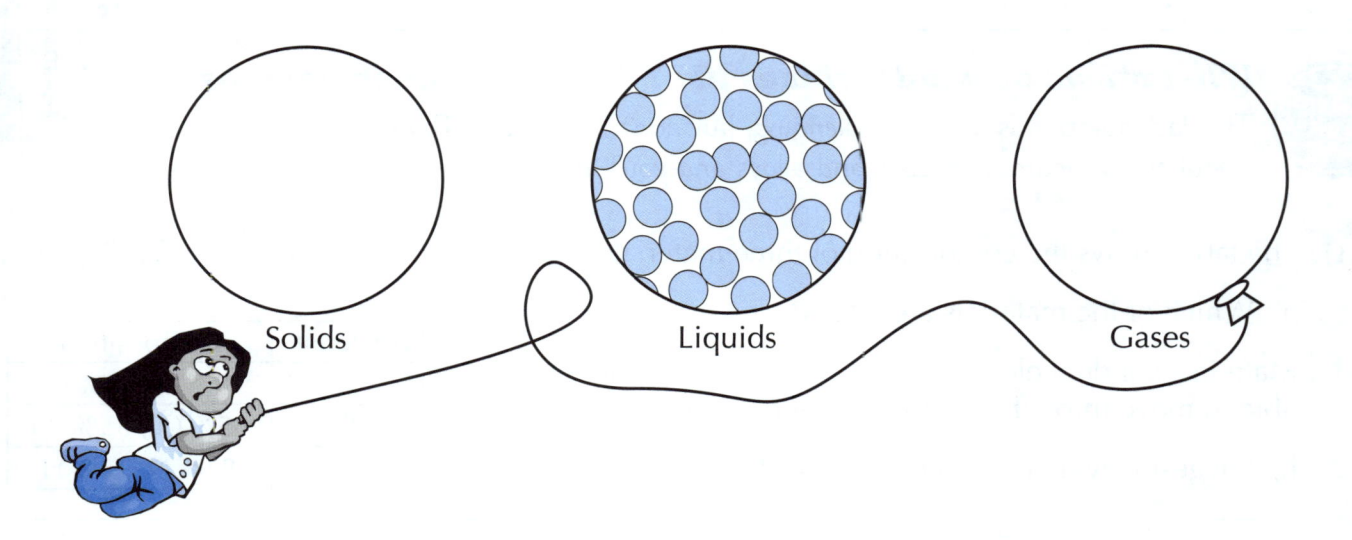

Solids, Liquids, Gases

Topic C2 — Bonding, Structure and Properties of Matter

Q3 Decide whether each of the statements below can describe a solid, a liquid and/or a gas.

	Solid	Liquid	Gas
The substance has a fixed shape.	☐	☐	☐
Particles are held in fixed positions.	☐	☐	☐
Particles are randomly arranged.	☐	☐	☐
The substance has a fixed volume.	☐	☐	☐

Q4 Look at this reaction equation: $2H_{2(g)} + O_{2(g)} \rightarrow 2H_2O_{(l)}$. What does (g) mean?

....

Q5 Circle the words in blue to make these sentences correct.

As a gas cools, its particles **gain / lose** energy. Forces **form / break** between the particles.

At the boiling point, the forces between the particles are **weak / strong** enough that the gas becomes a **liquid / solid**. When a liquid cools, the particles have **more / less** energy.

The forces between the particles become **stronger / weaker** until the particles are held in place and the liquid becomes a **solid / gas**.

Change of state — when the cheese on my toast melts...

NOW TRY THIS It's time to put this content to use with a quick question about melting and boiling points.

1) Euan has samples of four elements. The melting and boiling points for the four elements are shown in the table.

   Room temperature is 20 °C.

Element	Melting Point	Boiling Point
gallium	30 °C	2400 °C
bromine	−7 °C	59 °C
silver	962 °C	2162 °C
nitrogen	−210 °C	−196 °C

   a) What state will each of the four elements be in at room temperature?

   Normal body temperature is 37 °C. Euan holds some solid gallium in his hand for a while.

   b) What will Euan see happen to the gallium?

   c) Explain your answer to b) in terms of the energy of the gallium particles.

Topic C2 — Bonding, Structure and Properties of Matter

Topic C3 — Quantitative Chemistry

Relative Formula Mass

Just what you always wanted — a whole topic all about calculations in chemistry. The more practice you do, the easier it will get. Don't let me hold you back from jumping straight in...

Warm-Up

Circle the words in black to make this sentence correct.

The relative formula mass (A_r / M_r) of a compound is the sum of / difference between the relative formula / atomic masses of the atoms shown in the formula of the compound.

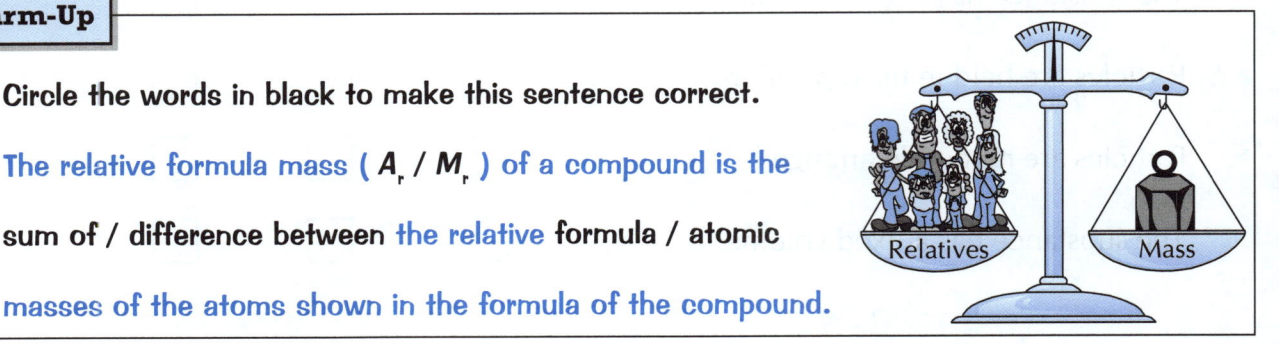

Q1 Nitric oxide is a gas. It has the formula NO. Find the relative formula mass of NO.

A_r of N = 14, A_r of O = 16

M_r = ... + ...

relative formula mass (M_r) = ...

Q2 Ammonia has the formula NH_3. What is the relative formula mass of NH_3? Tick the box.

A_r of N = 14, A_r of H = 1

M_r = ... + (.................... × 3)

= .... + ...

☐ 15   ☐ 16   ☐ 17   ☐ 18

Q3 Carbon dioxide is a greenhouse gas. It has the formula CO_2. Find the relative formula mass of CO_2.

A_r of C = 12, A_r of O = 16

M_r = ... + (.................... × 2)

= .... + ...

relative formula mass (M_r) = ...

Q4 Magnesium hydroxide has the formula Mg(OH)$_2$. What does the number 2 mean?

....

....

Q5 Aluminium hydroxide has the molecular formula Al(OH)$_3$.
Find the relative formula mass of Al(OH)$_3$.

A_r of Al = 27, A_r of O = 16, A_r of H = 1

relative formula mass (M_r) = ...

Q6 Water has the formula H$_2$O. Use the equation below to calculate the percentage mass of oxygen in water to the nearest whole number.

Don't let the equation put you off — just put the numbers in the right places.

$$\text{Percentage mass of oxygen in water} = \frac{A_r \text{ of oxygen} \times \text{number of atoms of oxygen}}{M_r \text{ of water}} \times 100$$

A_r of O = 16

M_r of H$_2$O = 18

percentage mass of oxygen = ... %

Roasted, chips, baked — relatives of mash...

NOW TRY THIS

Sometimes* you might be given a question that seems slightly different to usual — make sure you use all of the information that you've been given. *Now is one of those times.

1) Beryl has made a sample of beryllium chloride.
It is made up of beryllium (Be) and chlorine (Cl) and has the formula BeCl$_2$.
Use the information and the equation below to calculate the relative atomic mass of Be.

M_r of BeCl$_2$ = 80

A_r of Cl = 35.5

A_r of Be = M_r of BeCl$_2$ − (A_r of Cl × 2)

For this question you'll need to start from the relative formula mass and work backwards to calculate the relative atomic mass — use the equation given to you.

Topic C3 — Quantitative Chemistry

Conservation of Mass

Unless you're a wizard, it's unlikely you can make something out of nothing. That's because of conservation of mass, which comes with a fresh load of maths questions. What a treat.

Warm-Up

The statements below are about chemical reactions.
For each one, tick whether it is true or false.

	True	False
Atoms are made during a chemical reaction.	☐	☐
No atoms are lost during a chemical reaction.	☐	☐
There are the same number of atoms on each side of an equation.	☐	☐
The types of atoms can change in a reaction.	☐	☐

Q1 Sulfur reacts with oxygen to make sulfur dioxide. No other products are made.

16 g of sulfur reacts with 16 g of oxygen. What mass of sulfur dioxide is made?

☐ 8 g   ☐ 16 g   ☐ 24 g   ☐ 32 g

Q2 Calcium carbonate breaks down when it is heated.
This makes calcium oxide and carbon dioxide.

25 g of calcium carbonate is heated.
14 g of calcium oxide is made.

Calculate the mass of carbon dioxide made.

Fill in the numbers, then rearrange the equation.

.... = ... + mass of carbon dioxide

mass of carbon dioxide = ... g

Q3 Water is made from the reaction of hydrogen with oxygen.
The equation for this reaction is $2H_2 + O_2 \rightarrow 2H_2O$.

Explain how the equation shows mass is conserved in this reaction.

....

Topic C3 — Quantitative Chemistry

Q4 Magnesium hydroxide reacts with sulfuric acid to make magnesium sulfate and water.

2.9 g of magnesium hydroxide reacts with 4.9 g of sulfuric acid. 1.8 g of water is made.

Calculate the mass of magnesium sulfate made.

.... + ... = ... + mass of magnesium sulfate

mass of magnesium sulfate = ... g

Q5 When methane burns, it reacts with oxygen in the air. This makes carbon dioxide and water.

4 g of methane burns to make 11 g of carbon dioxide and 9 g of water.

What mass of oxygen did the methane react with?

mass of oxygen = ... g

Taking good care of revision notes — that's pass conservation...

NOW TRY THIS

It doesn't matter if you're looking at actual masses, or the number of atoms in the atomic and formula masses of a reaction — mass is always conserved.

1) Esme adds calcium to water to make calcium hydroxide and water.
   The equation for her reaction is $Ca_{(s)} + 2H_2O_{(l)} \rightarrow Ca(OH)_{2(aq)} + H_{2(g)}$

   A_r of Ca = 40, A_r of H = 1
   M_r of H_2O = 18, M_r of $Ca(OH)_2$ = 74

   a) Use the relative atomic masses and relative formula masses to show that mass is conserved in this reaction.

   In her reaction, 10.0 g of calcium reacts with 9.0 g of water. 0.5 g of hydrogen is produced.

   b) Calculate the mass of calcium hydroxide made.

   She carries out the reaction in an open flask on some scales. Bubbles are produced and the mass shown on the scales goes down.

   c) Why do you think the mass goes down?

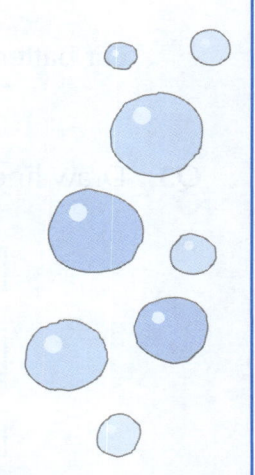

Topic C3 — Quantitative Chemistry

Topic C4 — Chemical Changes

Acids and Bases

There are some exciting reactions and colourful indicators coming up. A bit of colour would make this page look nicer, but I can only print things in blue. See the rainbow below. Sorry.

Warm-Up

The lower the pH of a solution, the more .... it is.   *alkaline*

The higher the pH of a solution, the more .... it is.   *acidic*

Q1 Use the words in the box to complete the paragraph about pH.

| indicator | 14 | acidity | less | 7 | colour | greater |

The pH scale measures the .... of a solution.

It can be tested using universal .... or using a pH probe.

The pH scale goes from 0 to .... A neutral solution has a pH of ....

Solutions of acids have pH values .... than 7.

Solutions of alkalis have pH values .... than 7.

Q2 Below are some substances with their pH values.
For each one, tick whether the substance is an acid, an alkali, or if it is neutral.

	acid	alkali	neutral
bleach — pH 12	☐	☐	☐
lemon juice — pH 3	☐	☐	☐
washing up liquid — pH 8	☐	☐	☐
pure water — pH 7	☐	☐	☐
car battery acid* — pH 1	☐	☐	☐

*There's a handy hint...

Q3 Draw lines to match the name of the acid to the type of salt it makes.

nitric acid   sulfate

hydrochloric acid   nitrate

sulfuric acid   chloride

Q4 What is the word equation for neutralisation?

.... + ... → .... + ...

[water] [base] [acid] [salt]

Q5 The words below are things made in the reaction between a metal carbonate and an acid. Use the clues to figure out the words.

This is a gas.   c__rb__n d__ox__d__

This is a neutral liquid.   w__t__r

This is an ionic compound.   s__lt

Q6 Circle the words in blue to make these sentences correct.

If something is soluble, that means it dissolves. If it's insoluble, it doesn't dissolve.

Copper chloride is a soluble salt that can be made by reacting **hydrochloric / sulfuric** acid with copper oxide. Copper oxide is a solid **soluble / insoluble** base. Add the solid to the **cold / warm** acid until no more reacts. Remove the excess solid by **sieving / filtering** the solution to produce a solution of the salt. Remove the water by **cooling / heating** the solution to produce pure salt crystals. Filter the crystals out of the solution and then dry them.

NOW TRY THIS

Acids — not as basic as alkalis...

Vinegar and sodium hydrogencarbonate — or as I like to call it, a volcanic eruption without too much disruption. Hey, looks like I'm a poet.

1) Christos is making a model volcano. He wants to use colourless vinegar (an acid with a pH of 3) and sodium hydrogencarbonate (a metal carbonate).

   He wants to test how he is going to get his volcano to erupt. He puts 150 cm³ of vinegar into a beaker and adds a few drops of universal indicator.

   a) What colour will the indicator be in the vinegar?

   He adds 10 g of sodium hydrogencarbonate to the vinegar. It produces a foam (lots of bubbles), which makes a huge mess.

   b) What gas is in the bubbles?

   Christos looks at the liquid left in the bottom of the beaker. He expects the liquid to be green.

   c) Explain why Christos expects the liquid to be green after the reaction.

   d) The liquid is blue. What do you think this means about the reaction?

Topic C4 — Chemical Changes

Reactions of Metals

Fun fact: some metals have such a vigorous reaction with water, they catch on fire.
Hopefully your reaction to this page won't be quite as explosive, otherwise it's gonna get messy...

Warm-Up

Circle the words in black to make these sentences correct.

When metals react with other substances, the metal atoms form **positive / negative** ions.

The **less / more** reactive a metal is, the more easily it forms ions.

The reactivity series lists metals in order of how **reactive / colourful** they are.

Q1 The reaction of potassium and water produces hydrogen gas and another product. What is the name of the other product?

☐ potassium chloride   ☐ Peter

☐ potassium hydroxide   ☐ sodium hydroxide

Q2 Complete the equations for the reaction of copper and oxygen.

Symbol Equation: 2 .... + ... ⟶ 2CuO

Word Equation: copper + oxygen ⟶ ....

Q3 Use the words in the box to complete the paragraph about metal extraction.

| extracted | reactive | oxides | unreactive |

Some metals are found in the Earth by themselves because they are ....

More .... metals are found as compounds, such as metal ....

The metal has to be .... from these compounds.

Q4 Which two non-metals are often included in the reactivity series?

....

Topic C4 — Chemical Changes

Q5 Draw lines to join each salt to the acid and metal you could use to make it.

Acids	Salts	Metals
	magnesium sulfate	iron
hydrochloric acid		
	zinc chloride	magnesium
sulfuric acid		
	iron sulfate	zinc

Q6 Use the reactivity series shown below to complete the table. One metal has been put in the table for you.

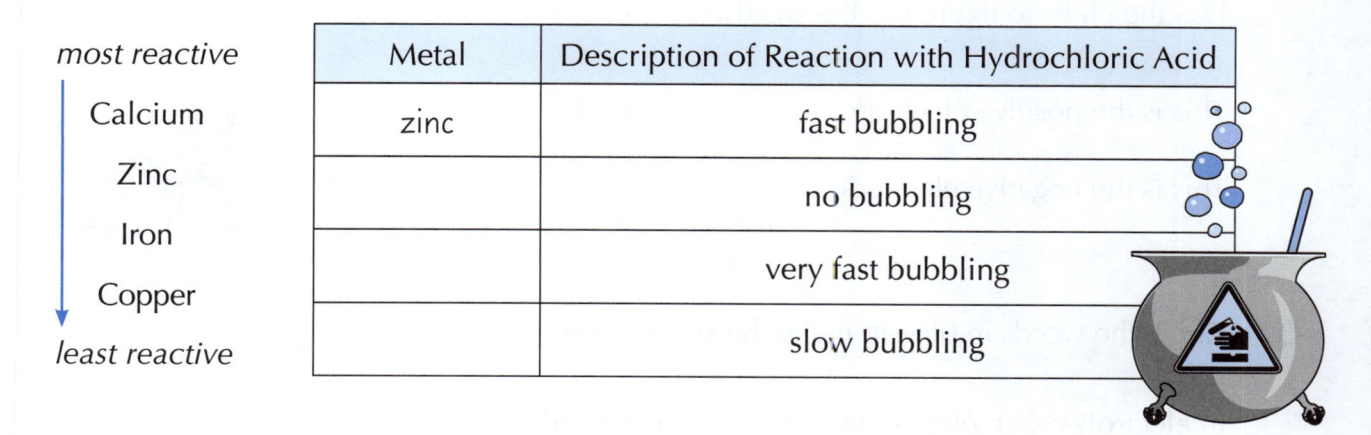

most reactive
Calcium
Zinc
Iron
Copper
least reactive

Metal	Description of Reaction with Hydrochloric Acid
zinc	fast bubbling
	no bubbling
	very fast bubbling
	slow bubbling

Q7 What is the word equation for the reaction of calcium with hydrochloric acid?

.... + ... → .... + ...

Catching on fire in water? Seems like a bit of an over-reaction to me...

NOW TRY THIS

The reactivity series is a pretty nifty little tool for predicting how a metal might react. Make sure you can remember and describe the different reactions.

1) For this question, you'll need to use the reactivity series from question 6.

Hassan does an experiment which shows iron doesn't react with water.

a) He says, "This proves zinc will not react with water either." Explain why Hassan is wrong.

b) Apart from iron, which metal can Hassan be sure doesn't react with water?

c) Hassan has a sample of magnesium. He wants to know where it would fit in the reactivity series given in question 6. Describe how he could use hydrochloric acid to do this.

Topic C4 — Chemical Changes

Electrolysis

Spoiler alert — splitting things using electricity isn't a superpower. You aren't going to see it in that new blockbuster superhero film. Don't let me stop you from finding out the truth — read on...

Warm-Up

Electrolysis can break down molten magnesium oxide into a metal and a gas.

What is the metal? ....

What is the gas? ....

Q1 The words below are the two electrodes in electrolysis, with the vowels removed. Use the clues to figure out the words.

This is the positive electrode.   __n__d__

This is the negative electrode.   c__th__d__

Q2 Circle the words in blue to make these sentences correct.

In electrolysis, an electric **current / field** is passed through an electrolyte.

Positive ions in the electrolyte move towards the **positive / negative** electrode.

Negative ions in the electrolyte move towards the **positive / negative** electrode.

The ions form uncharged **elements / electrodes**.

Q3 The statements below are about the electrolysis of a molten ionic compound. For each one, tick whether it is true or false.

	True	False
The ions in a molten ionic compound are free to move.	☐	☐
Metal ions move to the positive electrode.	☐	☐
The non-metal is formed at the positive electrode.	☐	☐
Molten ionic compounds always break up into their elements by electrolysis.	☐	☐

Topic C4 — Chemical Changes

Q4 Why can dissolved ionic compounds be electrolysed, but solid ionic compounds can't?

....

....

Q5 Fill in the crossword using the clues. One has been done for you.

Across

1) What gas bleaches damp litmus paper?

5) What is the negative ion formed when water breaks down?

6) What is produced at the anode in the electrolysis of molten lead bromide?

8) What is the name of a liquid or solution that conducts electricity?

Down

2) What is produced at the cathode in the electrolysis of molten lead bromide?

3) What is produced at the cathode in the electrolysis of molten sodium chloride?

4) What gas relights a glowing splint?

5) What gas makes a 'squeaky pop' with a lighted splint?

7) What is another word for unreactive?

Crossword filled entries:
- 1 Across: C_ _ _ _ _ (starts with C, 2 Down L)
- 5 Across: HYDROXIDE
- 6 Across: BR_ _
- 8 Across: E_E_ _R_ _
- 3 Down: S
- 4 Down: O
- 7 Down: I_E

Relight my glowing splint — a catchy disco classic...

NOW TRY THIS

Right, it's time to apply some of the lovely stuff covered on these pages — make sure you can describe the experimental set-up for the electrolysis of aqueous solutions.

1) Jemima is carrying out the electrolysis of an aqueous solution of copper chloride.

   a) In this reaction, copper forms at the cathode. What will Jemima see happen?

   Remember, 'aqueous' just means 'dissolved in water'.

   Chlorine gas is produced at the anode.

   b) What will Jemima see that shows a gas has been produced?

   c) Describe how Jemima could collect the chlorine gas.

   d) Describe how Jemima could carry out a gas test for chlorine. What result should she expect?

Topic C4 — Chemical Changes

Topic C5 — Energy Changes

Exothermic and Endothermic Reactions

Sometimes reactions are hot, sometimes reactions are cold, sometimes reactions go FIZZ... and sometimes you have to answer several pages of questions on energy changes. That's life, you see.

Warm-Up

In a chemical reaction, energy can't be made or
☐ destroyed. ☐ stored. ☐ moved around. ☐ recycled.

At the end of a chemical reaction, the total amount of energy in the universe is always
☐ increasing. ☐ decreasing. ☐ the same.

Q1 Use the words on the right to complete these sentences about energy changes.

An .... reaction is a reaction that gives out energy.

An .... reaction is a reaction that takes in energy.

exothermic

endothermic

Q2 Circle the words in blue to make these sentences correct.

Different chemicals store **different / equal** amounts of energy. Sometimes, the products of a reaction store more energy than the reactants. This means that the products take in energy from the **Sun / surroundings** during the reaction. But, if the products store less energy than the reactants, then the extra energy is **given out / created** during the reaction. So the overall amount of **reactants / energy** doesn't change.

Q3 Below are some statements about reactions. For each one, decide whether the statement is describing an exothermic or endothermic reaction.

	Exothermic	Endothermic
A reaction that makes the surroundings heat up.	☐	☐
A neutralisation reaction between an acid and an alkali.	☐	☐
A thermal decomposition reaction.	☐	☐
A combustion reaction.	☐	☐
A reaction that makes the surroundings cool down.	☐	☐

Q4 You can measure the temperature change of a reaction using the equipment below. Add labels to complete the diagram.

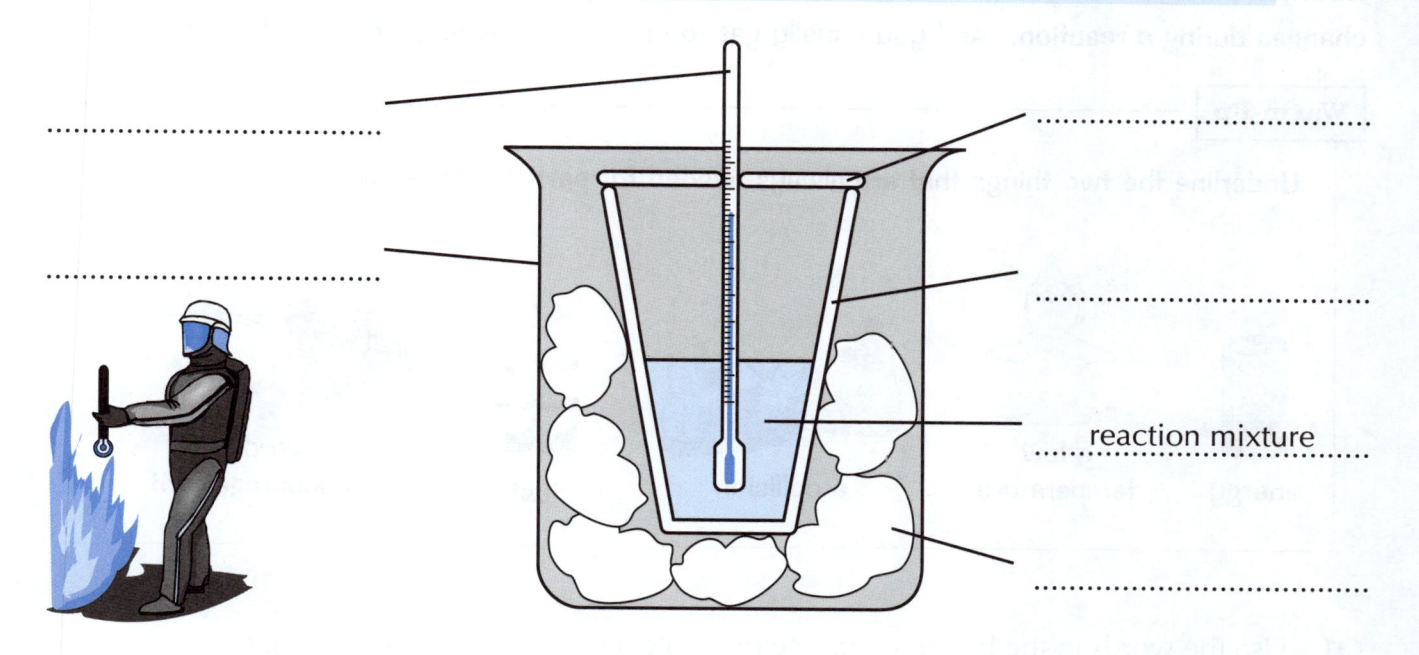

....

....

....

.... reaction mixture ....

....

Q5 A student measures the temperature change of a reaction. How can the student tell if the reaction is exothermic or endothermic?

....

....

You put the energy in, you take the energy out, you shake it all about...

NOW TRY THIS

Whoa, you've done a whole set of questions on energy changes. Don't turn around just yet though — here's an applied question for you to sink your teeth into. That's what it's all about.

1) Raissa measures the start and end temperature of five different reactions (A-E). Her results are shown in the table.

Reaction	A	B	C	D	E
Start temperature (°C)	19	22	21	25	21
End temperature (°C)	39	15	24	6	92

a) For each reaction, state whether it is exothermic or endothermic.

b) Which reaction had the greatest change in temperature?

Reaction D was between sodium carbonate and an acid. Raissa wants to know if the concentration of the acid affects the temperature change of this reaction.

c) What could Raissa do to find out if acid concentration affects the temperature change of reaction D?

Hand warmers are small packets that are held to warm up cold hands. Some hand warmers contain a chemical reaction that generates heat.

d) Which of the reactions has a temperature change that you think would be suitable in a hand warmer? Explain your answer.

Topic C5 — Energy Changes

Reaction Profiles

Reaction profiles aren't very thrilling, I'm afraid. But they are useful for showing you the energy changes during a reaction. And you usually get to do some sketching, so it's not all bad.

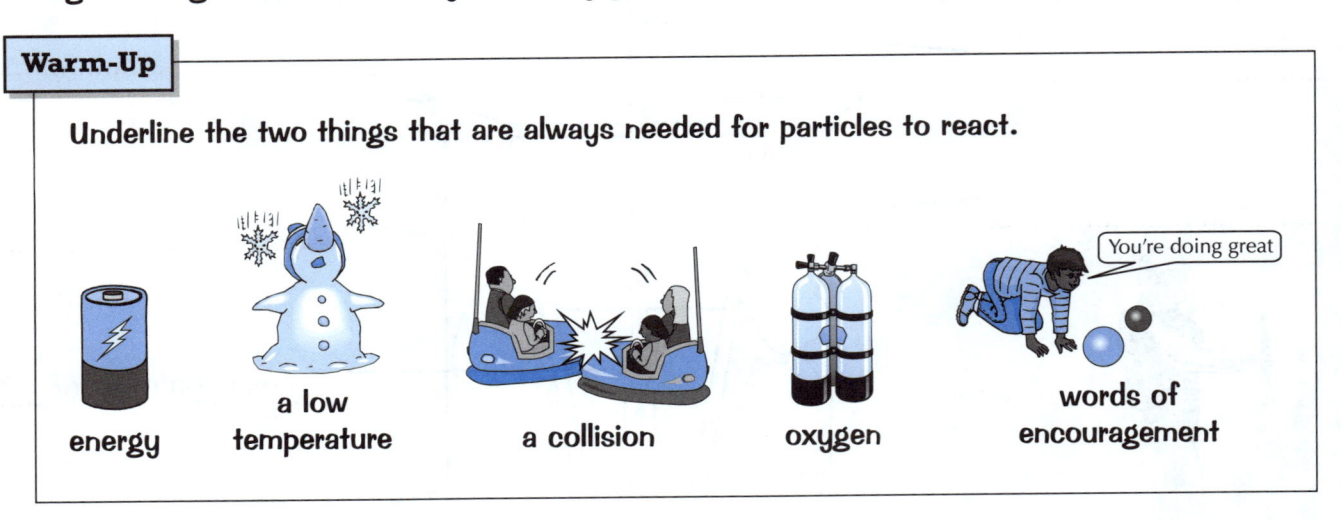

Warm-Up

Underline the two things that are always needed for particles to react.

energy | a low temperature | a collision | oxygen | words of encouragement

Q1 Use the words in the box to complete the sentences about activation energy.

| maximum | less | swap | more | collide | minimum |

The activation energy is the ……………… amount of energy the reactants need to have

to react when they ……………… with each other.

The greater the activation energy, the ……………… energy is needed to start the reaction.

Q2 Shaun carried out a reaction. The reaction profile is shown below.

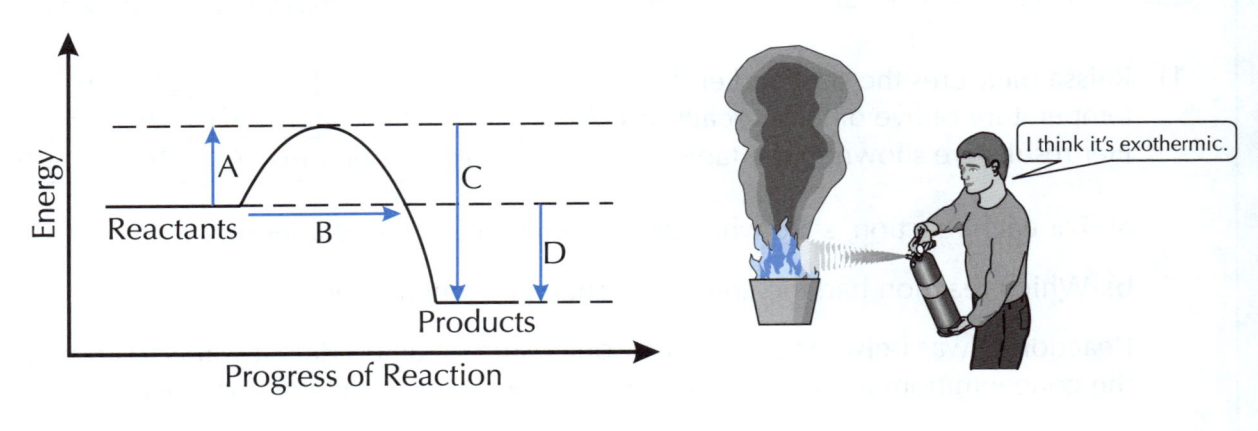

Which arrow (A-D) shows the activation energy of the reaction?

☐ A ☐ B ☐ C ☐ D

Which arrow (A-D) shows the overall energy change during the reaction?

☐ A ☐ B ☐ C ☐ D

Topic C5 — Energy Changes

Q3 How can you tell that the reaction profile in Q2 is for an exothermic reaction?

....

....

Q4 Kallum heats some calcium carbonate (CaCO₃). It breaks down to form calcium oxide (CaO) and carbon dioxide (CO₂). This reaction is endothermic. Complete the reaction profile for this reaction below. Label the activation energy and the overall energy change.

Don't forget to label the axes.

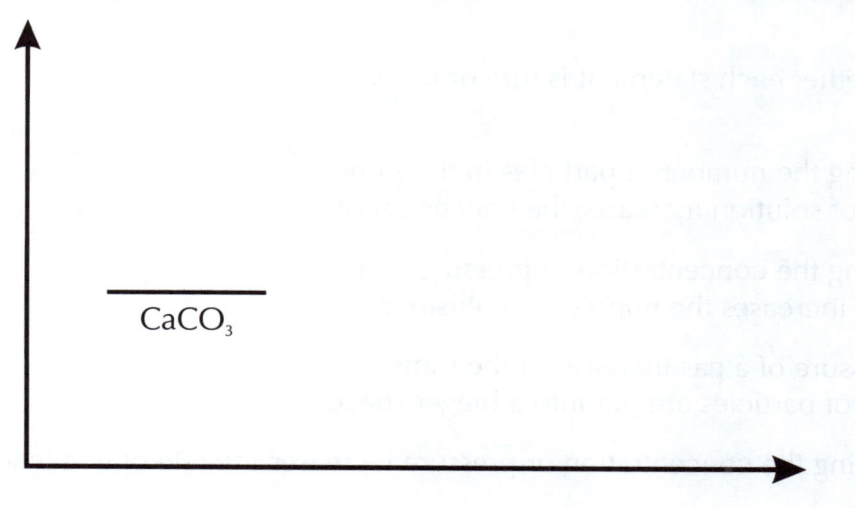

CaCO₃

Reactions are like a lot of things in life, really...

...You have to put some energy in before you get the reward. Hang in there, because there's only one more question to go on this topic. Then you can get more energy from a biscuit.

1) Two reactions, X and Y, were carried out at 45 °C. Their reaction profiles are shown below.

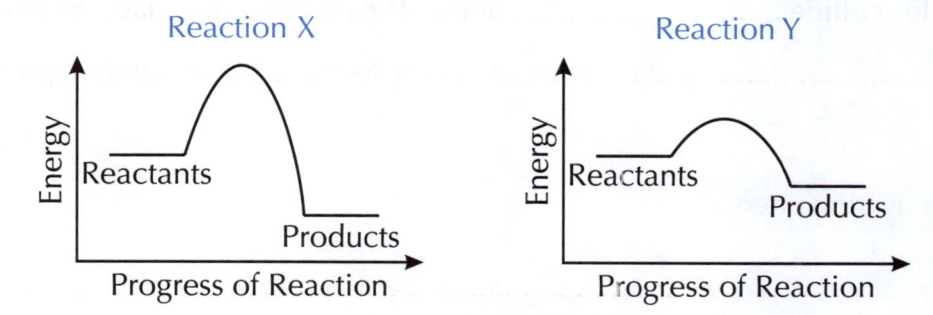

Reaction X — Energy vs Progress of Reaction: Reactants, Products

Reaction Y — Energy vs Progress of Reaction: Reactants, Products

a) Which reaction, X or Y, had a greater activation energy? Explain your answer.

b) Which reaction, X or Y, gave out the most energy? Explain your answer.

Topic C5 — Energy Changes

Topic C6 — The Rate and Extent of Chemical Change

Rates of Reaction

Rates of reaction are all about how quickly you can make something. My rate for Sunday morning breakfasts is half as quick as my running-late-Monday-morning breakfasts. I'll never learn...

> **Warm-Up**
>
> Which of these sentences about collision theory is correct?
>
> ☐ Collision theory says that particles never collide.
>
> ☐ Collision theory says that a reaction can only take place when particles collide with enough energy.
>
> ☐ Collision theory says that a reaction will always take place.

Q1 Tick whether each statement is true or false.

	True	False
Increasing the number of particles in the same volume of solution increases the concentration.	☐	☐
Increasing the concentration or pressure of a reaction increases the number of collisions.	☐	☐
The pressure of a gas increases if the same number of particles are put into a bigger space.	☐	☐
Decreasing the concentration or pressure increases the rate of a reaction.	☐	☐

Q2 Use the words in the box to complete these sentences about particles.

| more   energy   slower   faster   less   collisions |

When temperature increases, particles move .... This means that the particles collide .... often. The particles also have more energy, so more .... have enough energy to make the reaction happen.

Q3 What is activation energy?

....

....

Topic C6 — The Rate and Extent of Chemical Change

Q4 Circle the words in blue to make these sentences about catalysts correct.

A catalyst is a substance that **speeds up / slows down** a reaction.

All / none of the catalyst gets used up in the reaction. A catalyst changes

the way a reaction happens so the reaction has a **higher / lower** activation energy.

Enzymes are **magical / biological** catalysts that affect reactions in living things.

Q5 Diagrams **A-D** show the particles of a reaction under different conditions. Circle the diagram that shows the conditions that would give the fastest rate.

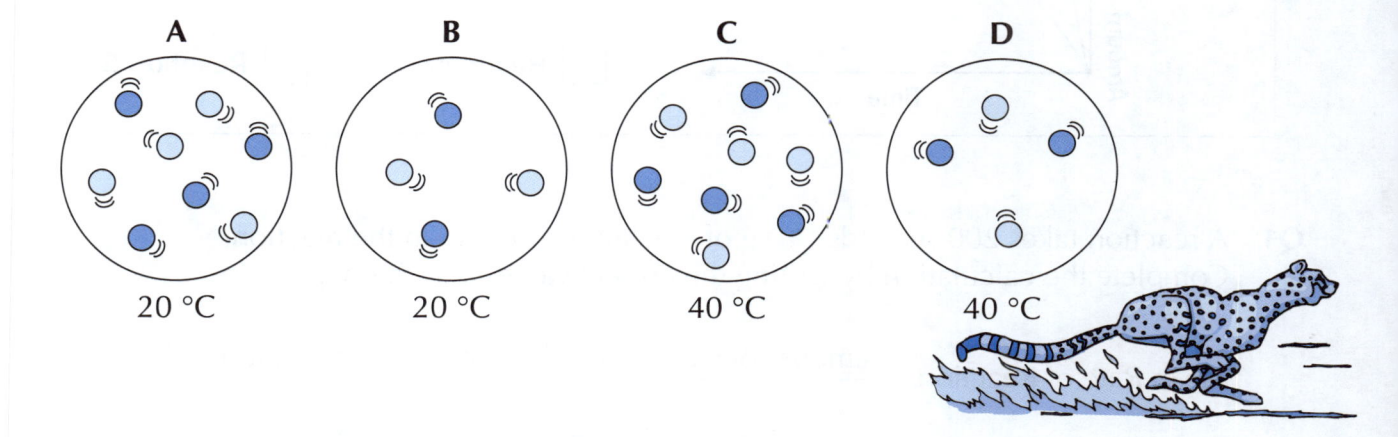

A   B   C   D
20 °C   20 °C   40 °C   40 °C

Q6 How does increasing the surface area of a solid reactant increase the rate of reaction?

....

....

Measuring rates of reaction — raters gonna rate...

NOW TRY THIS

Rates of revision: the faster you get through this final question, the faster you can ~~throw this book at someone to test their reaction rate~~ move onto the next page...

1) Charis places a conical flask on top of a piece of paper with a black cross on it. She adds sodium thiosulfate and hydrochloric acid to the flask. They are both clear solutions that react to form a yellow precipitate of sulfur.

   A precipitate is a solid product.

   She is investigating the rate of reaction.

   a) How can the black cross be used to show reaction rate?

   She repeats the reaction with a sodium thiosulfate solution of a higher concentration. She keeps everything else the same. The rate of the reaction increases.

   b) Explain why the rate of reaction increases.

Topic C6 — The Rate and Extent of Chemical Change

és
Calculating Rates of Reaction

There's just one key formula to use on this page. Unfortunately, it comes with a side of graphs, but they can be easy to understand if you know the formula. Don't hang about, jump in...

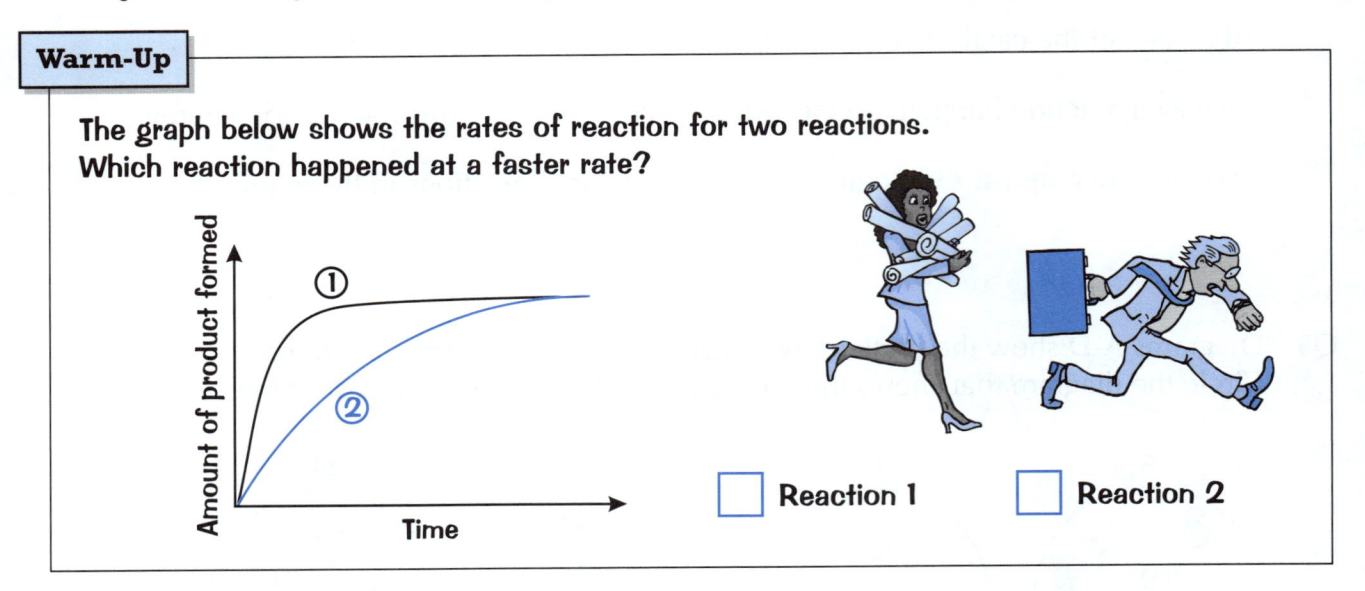

Warm-Up

The graph below shows the rates of reaction for two reactions.
Which reaction happened at a faster rate?

☐ Reaction 1   ☐ Reaction 2

Q1 A reaction takes 200 seconds. 10 g of reactant is used up in the reaction. Complete the calculation by writing the correct value in each box.

Mean Rate of Reaction = $\dfrac{\text{amount of reactant used (or amount product formed)}}{\text{time}}$

= ☐/☐ = ☐ g/s

Q2 The graph shows the volume of gas produced by a reaction. Fill in the blanks on the right and calculate the mean rate of reaction.

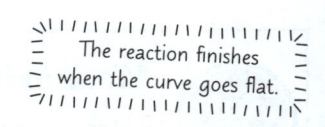

The reaction finishes when the curve goes flat.

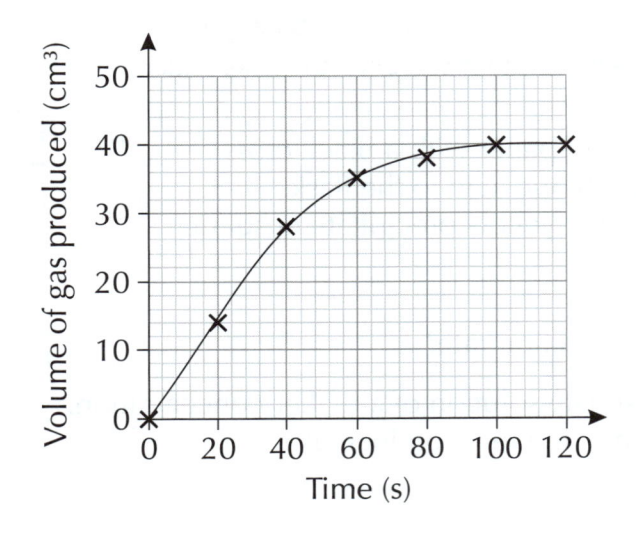

Time taken for reaction to finish = ... s

Volume of product made = ... cm^3

Mean Rate = ☐/☐

= ☐ cm^3/s

Topic C6 — The Rate and Extent of Chemical Change

Q3 A student used the gas syringe on the right to collect the gas given off by a reaction. The reaction took 45 seconds. What is the volume of gas in the syringe? Calculate the mean rate of this reaction.

Volume of gas = ... cm³

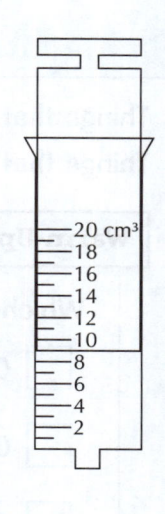

mean rate of reaction = ... cm³/s

Q4 The graph shows the mass of reactant used in a reaction against time. Draw a line of best fit and describe how the rate of reaction changes between 0 and 60 seconds.

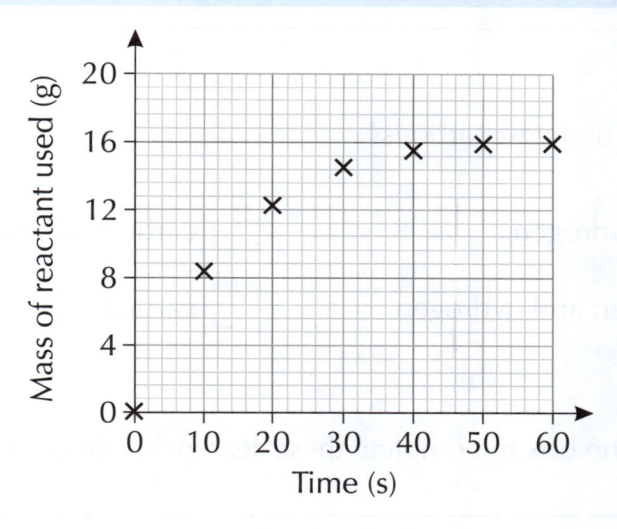

....

....

Marble chips — the crunchiest side dish...

NOW TRY THIS You might be given some information about a reaction and asked to draw a graph of the results. (In fact, you will definitely be asked to draw a graph in 5, 4, 3...)

1) Ethan is measuring the rate of reaction for an experiment. He adds marble chips to hydrochloric acid which forms carbon dioxide gas.

   a) Describe how Ethan could measure the volume of gas given off in his reaction.

   Ethan's results are shown in the table on the right.

   b) Find the mean rate of reaction (in cm³/s) for the first minute.

   c) Draw a graph of Ethan's results, with time on the x-axis and volume of gas on the y-axis. Include a line of best fit.

Time (s)	Volume of gas (cm³)
0	0
15	6.0
30	11.0
45	14.5
60	18.0
75	19.5
90	20.0

Topic C6 — The Rate and Extent of Chemical Change

Topic C7 — Organic Chemistry

Hydrocarbons and Crude Oil

Things that organic chemistry isn't: chemistry of church instruments or chemistry of body parts.
Things that organic chemistry is: the super exciting chemistry of compounds containing carbon...

Warm-Up

Which of these statements about crude oil are correct?

☐ Crude oil is a fossil fuel found in rocks.

☐ Crude oil will never run out.

☐ Crude oil is formed mainly from the remains of plankton.

☐ Crude oil is made up of one type of hydrocarbon.

Plankton are tiny living plants and animals which float around in oceans.

Crikey!

Q1 What atoms make up hydrocarbons?

☐ carbon and hydrogen ☐ carbon and oxygen

☐ carbon, oxygen and hydrogen ☐ carbon only

Q2 Use the words in the box to complete these sentences about the properties of hydrocarbons.

| more | less | higher | length | lower | colour |

As the .... of the carbon chain changes, the properties of the hydrocarbons change.

The shorter the carbon chain, the .... the boiling point.

The longer the carbon chain, the .... flammable the hydrocarbon is.

The shorter the carbon chain, the .... runny (less viscous) a hydrocarbon is.

Q3 Which of these are alkanes?

☐ C_6H_{14} ☐ C_3H_6 ☐ C_2H_6

☐ H₂C=CH₂ ☐ H–C(H)(H)–O–H ☐ H–C–C–C–C–C–H (pentane structural formula)

Topic C7 — Organic Chemistry

Q4 What is the general formula for alkanes?

....

Q5 Draw lines to match the displayed formulas to the names of the alkanes.

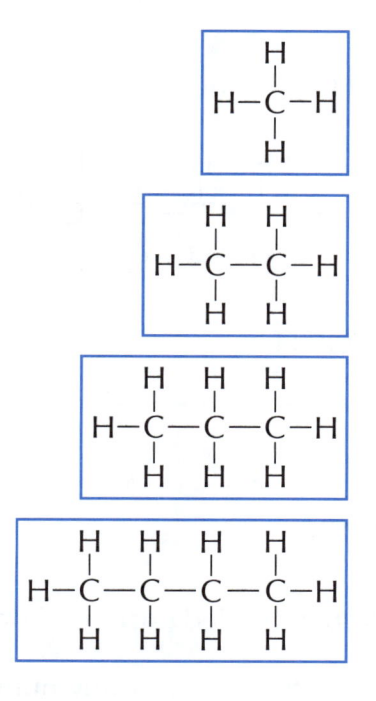

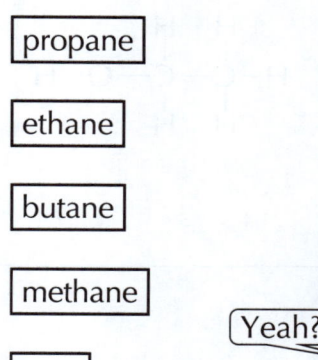

[CH₄ structure]
[C₂H₆ structure]
[C₃H₈ structure]
[C₄H₁₀ structure]

propane
ethane
butane
methane
Jane

Q6 Complete these equations for the complete combustion of propane.

Make sure you check that the symbol equation is balanced — you'll need to balance the water.

Words: .... + oxygen ⟶ .... + water

Symbols: C_3H_8 + 5 .... ⟶ $3CO_2$ + ...

Which alkane is used to make sheets of glass? Windowpane...

NOW TRY THIS

It's time to use that sweet alkane knowledge of yours to answer one more question. Unknown compounds look scary, but questions like these are all about applying your knowledge.

1) Decane and icosane are alkanes.
   Decane has the formula $C_{10}H_{22}$ and icosane has the formula $C_{20}H_{42}$.

   a) Which of the alkanes will have the higher boiling point?

   Malik wants to use one of the alkanes as a fuel.

   b) Which of the alkanes will be more flammable?

   One of the alkanes is a solid at room temperature. The other is a liquid.

   c) Which alkane do you think is a solid at room temperature? Explain your answer.

Topic C7 — Organic Chemistry

Using Hydrocarbons

Hydrocarbons aren't just things to fill exams with. They have some pretty important real-life uses. You need to know how hydrocarbons are separated and sorted to be more useful.

Warm-Up

Circle the compounds below that are hydrocarbons.

C_2H_4 C_3H_8

[structural formula of ethanol: H-C(H,H)-C(H,H)-O-H]   [structural formula of methane: H-C(H,H)-H]   [structural formula of butane: H-C(H,H)-C(H,H)-C(H,H)-C(H,H)-H]

H_2O CH_3COOH

Q1 Circle the words in blue to make these sentences correct.

Fractional distillation is used to separate crude oil into parts called **portions / fractions**. Each of these parts contains a mixture of hydrocarbons with **a similar / any** number of carbon atoms. Most of the hydrocarbons in crude oil are **alkanes / alkenes**.

Q2 Use the words in the box to complete these sentences about cracking.

| more | high | smaller | low | less | larger |

There is a .... demand for fuels with small molecules. Long-chain alkanes can be cracked to make .... , more useful alkanes. Cracking also makes alkenes — these are .... reactive than alkanes.

'Cracked' just means split up.

Q3 Give one use of alkenes.

....

Topic C7 — Organic Chemistry

Q4 The names of five fuels made from crude oil are hidden in this wordsearch. Find the names. The first letters of each fuel are given below.

1) P...
2) K...
3) H...
4) L...
5) D...

H	K	Q	W	O	A	X	N	D	H	Z	M
M	E	U	K	C	U	D	L	I	U	G	K
D	Y	A	J	C	B	E	R	E	A	F	B
D	O	N	V	E	N	C	S	S	F	L	N
A	L	S	R	Y	H	P	I	E	T	S	T
F	A	K	D	T	F	Q	J	L	P	G	A
E	P	S	G	M	N	U	T	O	E	M	I
K	E	R	O	S	E	N	E	I	T	Y	C
Y	R	W	N	L	I	V	P	L	R	T	R
A	S	G	O	H	J	O	B	W	O	L	S
S	B	I	Z	X	C	V	I	V	L	I	U
R	E	N	T	E	T	G	R	E	D	E	L

Fractional distillation — separating quarters from halves...

NOW TRY THIS

Have a think back to the previous couple of pages — the properties of hydrocarbons are really important when thinking about fractional distillation.

1) The diagram on the right shows a fractionating column used to separate the fractions of crude oil.

   The crude oil mixture is heated until most of it turns into a gas. The gases enter at the bottom of the column and cool as they travel up. The different fractions (A-F) turn back into liquids at different temperatures, so are collected at different points in the column.

   a) Which fraction has hydrocarbons with the lowest boiling points?

   b) Which fraction has hydrocarbons with the longest carbon chain lengths?

   c) Fractions B and D are both used as fuels. Which do you think is more flammable? Explain why.

   d) Fractions C and E are both liquids at room temperature. Which do you think is more runny? Explain why.

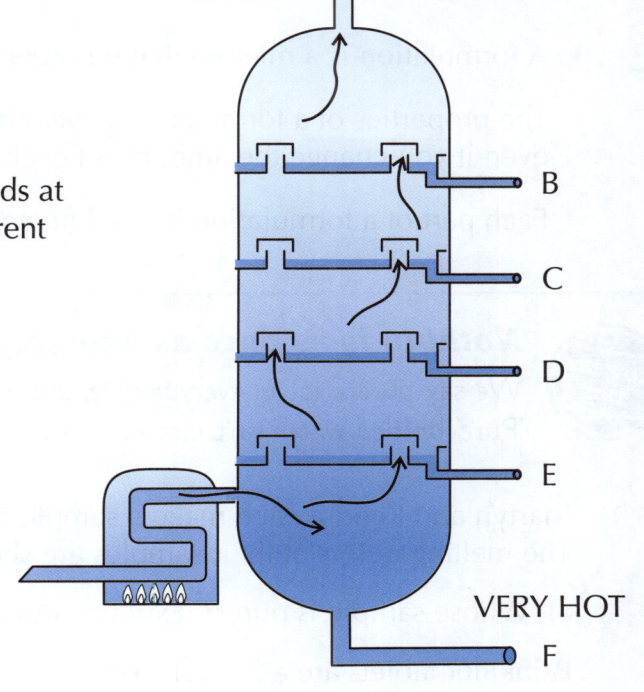

Topic C7 — Organic Chemistry

Topic C8 — Chemical Analysis

Purity and Formulations

Formulations are examples of mixtures. Formulations and other mixtures aren't chemically pure — in chemistry, pure substances only contain one compound or element all the way through.

Warm-Up

Circle the things that are chemically pure.

oxygen   cheese   paint   orange juice   gold   air

Q1 Use the words in the box to complete the paragraph about purity.

| closer   specific   range   pure   random   group |

Pure substances melt and boil at .... temperatures. You can tell how pure a substance is by comparing its melting point to that of the .... substance. The .... the measured value is to the actual melting point, the purer the sample is. Impurities cause the sample to melt across a .... of temperatures.

Q2 Are these statements about formulations true or false?

	True	False
A formulation is a mixture that has been designed for a particular use.	☐	☐
The properties of a formulation never change, even if you change the amounts of each ingredient.	☐	☐
Each part of a formulation has a different purpose.	☐	☐

Nothing is as pure as cute puppy videos...

We say pure a lot in everyday life, but we don't mean chemically pure. 'Pure' bottled water isn't just water molecules — it has other substances in it too.

1) Martyn and Kendra each make a sample of a compound used as a painkiller. The melting points of their samples are shown in the table.

   a) Whose sample is purer? Explain your answer.

Sample	Melting point (°C)
Martyn	162-166
Kendra	169

   Painkiller tablets are a formulation.

   b) Suggest a reason why other ingredients are added to painkiller tablets.

Topic C9 — Chemistry of the Atmosphere

Climate Change and Pollution

This is the second-to-last chemistry topic of the book, and there's only one page of questions. Don't go thinking this stuff isn't important though, it's a pretty hot topic right now...

Warm-Up

Which of these statements about greenhouse gases is correct?
- [ ] Greenhouse gases produce heat by themselves.
- [ ] Greenhouse gases keep the Earth warm enough to support life.

Which of these gases is *not* a greenhouse gas?
- [ ] methane
- [ ] carbon dioxide
- [ ] oxygen
- [ ] water vapour

Q1 Circle the words in blue to make these sentences correct.

Human activity is **increasing / decreasing** the amount of greenhouse gases in the atmosphere. Scientists believe that this will cause an **increase / decrease** in the temperature of the atmosphere and that this will result in global **language / climate** change.

Q2 Use the words in the box to complete the paragraph about carbon footprints.

| reducing | total | life | increasing |

A carbon footprint is a measure of the .... amount of carbon dioxide and other greenhouse gases released over the full .... cycle of something. A carbon footprint can be reduced by .... the amount of greenhouse gases given out by a process.

Q3 Draw lines to match the pollutants with the problems they can cause.

particulates	fainting and comas (or even death)
sulfur dioxide	breathing problems and global dimming
carbon monoxide	acid rain and breathing problems

Topic C9 — Chemistry of the Atmosphere

Topic C10 — Using Resources

Finite and Renewable Resources

"Waste not, want not" — that's what my gran always says. I'm not sure exactly what it means, but I think it's something to do with making good use of resources...

Warm-Up

Which of these are renewable resources? Circle the correct answers.

gold   wool   paper   petrol

Q1 What is the difference between a finite resource and a renewable resource?

....

....

Q2 Which of these sentences about sustainable development is correct?

☐ Sustainable development means continuing to extract resources at the current rate to make sure that development continues at the same rate.

☐ Sustainable development means thinking about the needs of people today without damaging the lives of people in the future.

☐ Sustainable development means not using any resources so that the people can use them in the future instead.

Now Try This

Recycling does not mean getting back on your bike...

This stuff is useful for real life as well as for your chemistry exams.
If we all reduce, reuse and recycle as much as we can, that's good news for the planet.

1) *Clara's Ginger Pop* is a soft drinks company. The company sells ginger beer in glass bottles and metal cans. The bottles and cans are made by the company.

   a) The company starts paying supermarkets to collect and return their empty bottles to be reused. Explain why the company might save money by reusing the bottles, even though it has to pay to get them back.

   b) *Clara's Ginger Pop* makes its cans from newly-produced metal. Give one way that extracting new metals can damage the environment.

   c) The company wants to start using recycled metal instead. Describe one advantage of recycling used metal cans instead of throwing them away.

Potable Water

Water is pretty important stuff. We need to make sure we've got enough clean, safe water for everyone to drink. And wash with. And have massive water-pistol battles with...

Warm-Up

Below are some statements about types of water.
Tick whether each statement is true or false.

	True	False
Water that is safe to drink must be chemically pure.	☐	☐
Fresh water can come from lakes and rivers.	☐	☐
Most of the UK's drinking water is made by treating sea water.	☐	☐

Q1 Use words from the box to complete the sentences below.

| sterilised | desalinated | potable | filtered |

Fresh water must be treated to make it .... (safe to drink).

The water is .... to remove any solid particles.

The water is then .... using chlorine, ozone or ultraviolet light.

Some countries don't have enough fresh water, so they use .... sea water.

That was refreshing...

I hope the page is going swimmingly for you so far. Make sure you know all of the water treatment steps before you dive into one more question about water...

1) Bianca wants to purify a sample of sea water.

   a) First, she tests the pH of the sea water.
      Suggest one way she could do this.

   b) She finds that the pH of the sea water is 8.
      What should she do to make the sea water neutral?

   c) The sea water contains dissolved salts.
      The diagram shows the equipment
      Bianca uses to purify the sea water.
      Describe how she can use the equipment
      to separate the water from the salts.

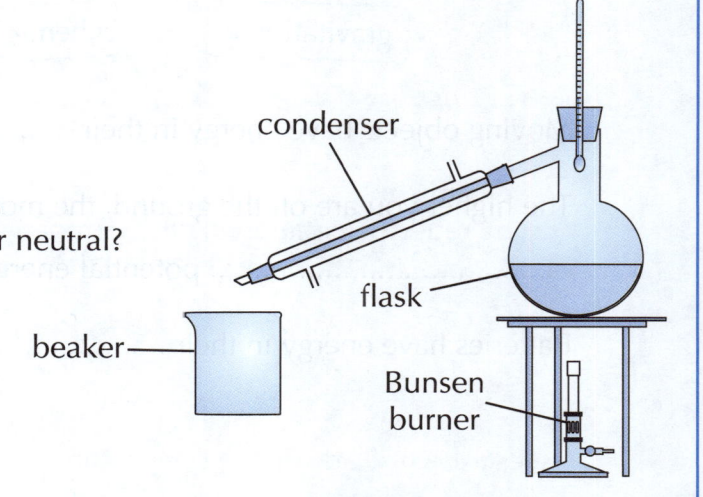

Topic C10 — Using Resources

Topic P1 — Energy

Energy Stores and Energy Transfers

Energy stores are tricky because you can't see them. But pretty much anything that happens, from moving your arm to heating up your leftover pizza involves energy moving between stores...

Warm-Up

Put a cross through each bucket that is not correctly labelled with a type of energy store.

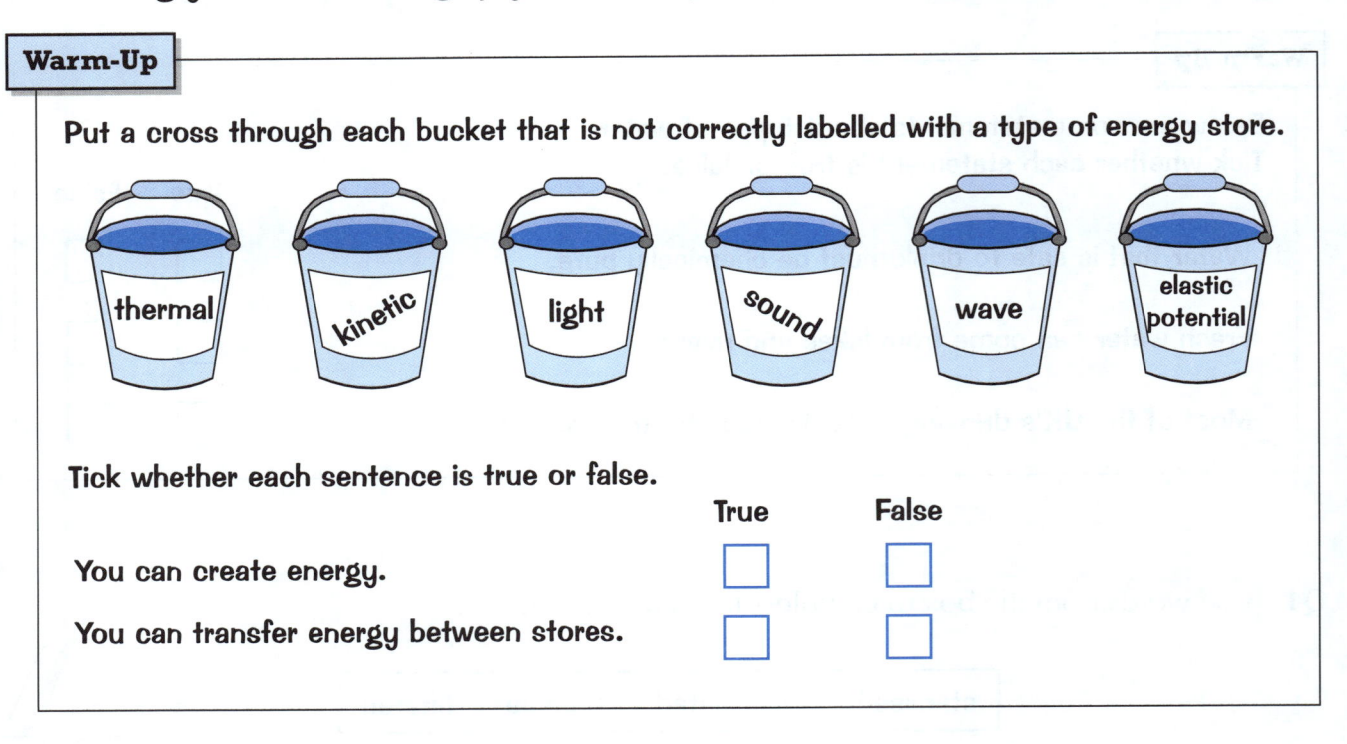

thermal | kinetic | light | sound | wave | elastic potential

Tick whether each sentence is true or false.

	True	False
You can create energy.	☐	☐
You can transfer energy between stores.	☐	☐

Q1 A stretched elastic band is released. It travels across the room. Circle words in blue to make the sentence correct.

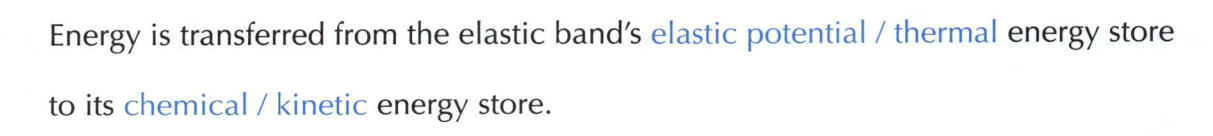

Energy is transferred from the elastic band's elastic potential / thermal energy store

to its chemical / kinetic energy store.

Q2 Choose from the words below to complete the sentences.

gravitational   chemical   kinetic

Moving objects have energy in their .... energy store.

The higher you are off the ground, the more energy you have in your

.... potential energy store.

Batteries have energy in their .... energy store.

Q3 Viv puts a spoon in her soup. The spoon warms up.

How is energy transferred from the soup to the spoon?

☐ electrically ☐ mechanically ☐ by heating

Q4 A car driver applies the brakes and the car slows down.
Use words from the box to complete the sentences.

| mechanical | force | kinetic | thermal |

The car slows down because a .... acts.

Energy is transferred from the .... energy store of the wheels

to the .... energy store of the brakes and the surroundings.

This is a .... energy transfer.

Q5 Which of the following is true?

☐ A system is an energy store. ☐ A system is an object or a group of objects.

☐ A system is a type of energy transfer. ☐ A system is force.

Q6 What is a closed system?

....

....

NOW TRY THIS

I hope your energy stores aren't completely empty...

There's just one question left to see if you really know your stuff.
It might make you fancy a chippy tea though.

1) A vulture steals a chip and flies away with it.
Energy is transferred to the kinetic energy store of the vulture's wings.

   a) Which energy store was this energy transferred from?

   The vulture drops the chip from high in the sky. It falls.

   b) Which of the chip's energy stores is energy transferred **away from**?

   c) Which of the chip's energy stores is energy transferred **to**?

Topic P1 — Energy

Heating and Unwanted Energy Transfers

It's lucky that energy can be transferred by heating, or it'd be really hard to make a cup of tea.

Warm-Up

An object is heated, causing its temperature to change.
Circle words in black to make the sentences below correct.

Heating transfers energy to the magnetic / thermal energy store of the object.

This makes its temperature increase / decrease.

Q1 Choose from the blue values to complete the definition of specific heat capacity.

| 1 g | 1 kg | 1 °C | 100 °C |

Specific heat capacity is the amount of energy needed to

raise the temperature of .... of a material by ....

Q2 Houses can be built to minimise the rate energy is transferred out of the house by heating. Complete the labels to show two ways of doing this.

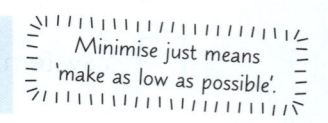

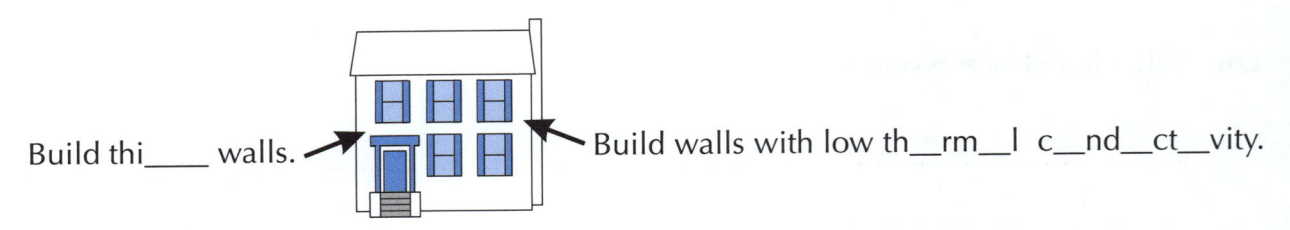

Minimise just means 'make as low as possible'.

Build thi____ walls.

Build walls with low th__rm__l c__nd__ct__vity.

Q3 Look at the electric kettle on the right.
Use some of the blue words to fill in the gaps to show the energy transfers when water is heated in this kettle.

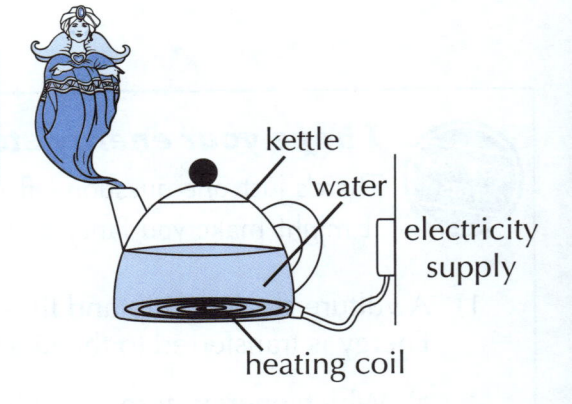

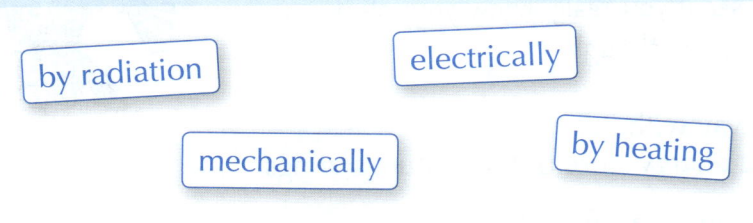

by radiation   electrically   mechanically   by heating

Energy is transferred ....

Energy is transferred ....

Electricity supply → Thermal energy store of the heating coil → Thermal energy store of the water

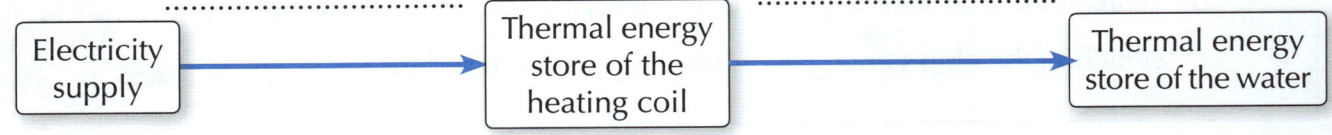

Topic P1 — Energy

Q4 Energy can be dissipated. What does this mean?

☐ It can be destroyed.   ☐ It can be transferred to less useful energy stores.

☐ It can be transferred usefully.   ☐ It can be created.

Q5 Liquid A has a higher specific heat capacity than liquid B. There is 1 kg of each liquid. Which of the following is true?

☐ Increasing liquid A's temperature by 1 °C takes more energy.

☐ Increasing liquid B's temperature by 1 °C takes more energy.

Q6 A cyclist lubricates the chain of her bike using oil. Explain how this affects the amount of energy dissipated due to friction when the bike is ridden.

....

....

Things are really hotting up now...

NOW TRY THIS

The sea stays chilly even when the weather is hot. That's because water has a high specific heat capacity and there's a lot of it, so it takes loads of energy to warm it up even a little bit.

1) Amira uses a heater to transfer 500 J of energy to the thermal energy store of a 1 kg block of metal. The block is surrounded by insulation. She measures and records the starting and finishing temperature of the block. She repeats the experiment with a 1 kg block of a different metal.

Metal	Starting temperature (°C)	Finishing temperature (°C)
Metal 1	20	24
Metal 2	20	22

a) Calculate the temperature change for each metal.

b) Which metal has the highest specific heat capacity? ← *Think about how much energy must have been needed for each 1 °C temperature rise for each metal.*

c) Amira repeated the experiment with a different metal. Give two things she kept the same in the experiments to make it a fair test.

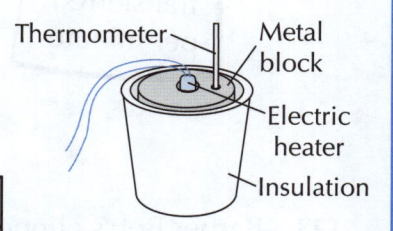

Topic P1 — Energy

Power and Efficiency

Powerful, efficient things transfer energy quickly without wasting much of it. They're really great. I wish I was powerful and efficient getting out of bed in the morning. But I move like a sloth.

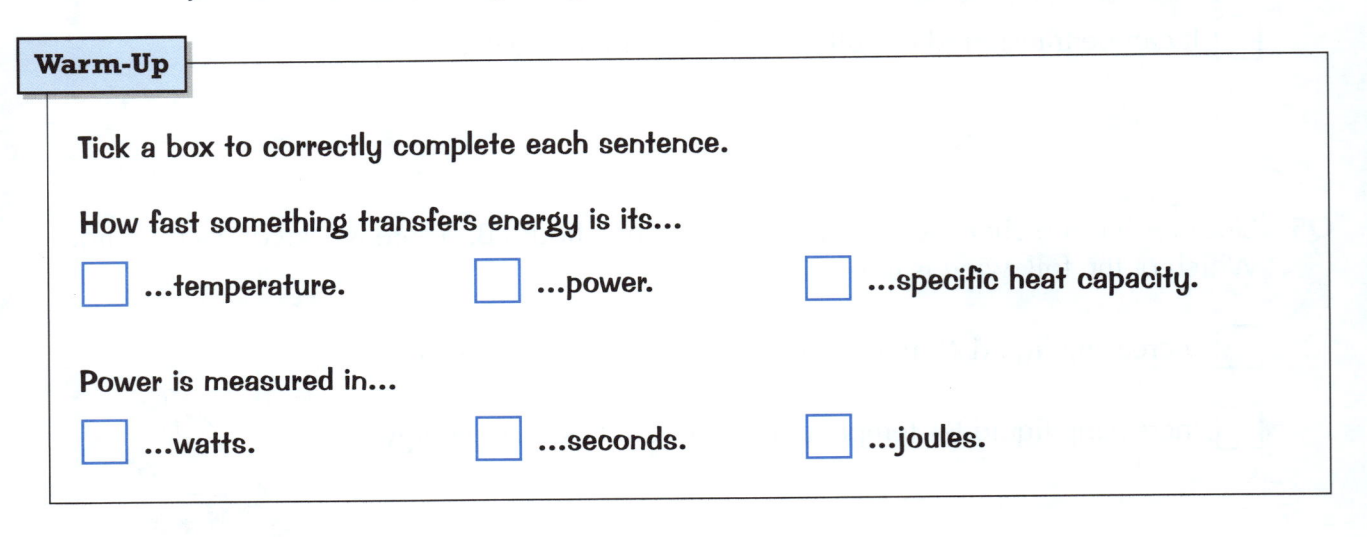

Warm-Up

Tick a box to correctly complete each sentence.

How fast something transfers energy is its...

☐ ...temperature.   ☐ ...power.   ☐ ...specific heat capacity.

Power is measured in...

☐ ...watts.   ☐ ...seconds.   ☐ ...joules.

Q1 Choose from the words in the boxes to complete the fact below.

| kilogram | joule | newton | | day | hour | second |

1 watt = 1 .... of energy transferred per ....

Q2 Circle the machine below that has the highest power.

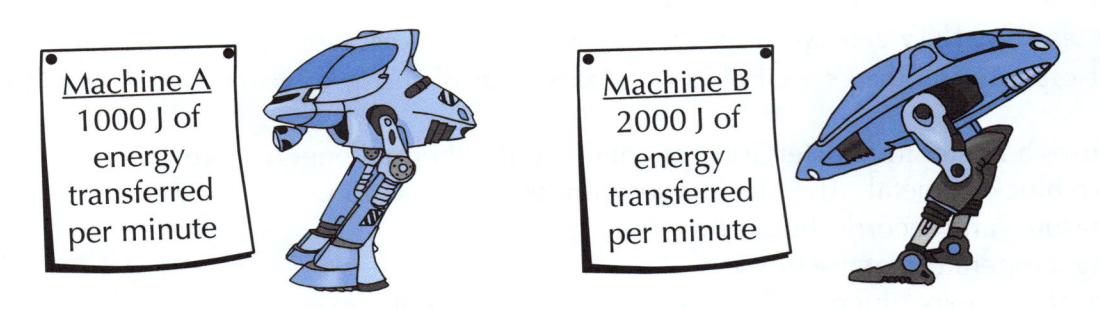

Machine A — 1000 J of energy transferred per minute

Machine B — 2000 J of energy transferred per minute

Q3 Barber Bob's clippers transfer 800 joules of energy in 20 seconds. Calculate their power using the equation below.

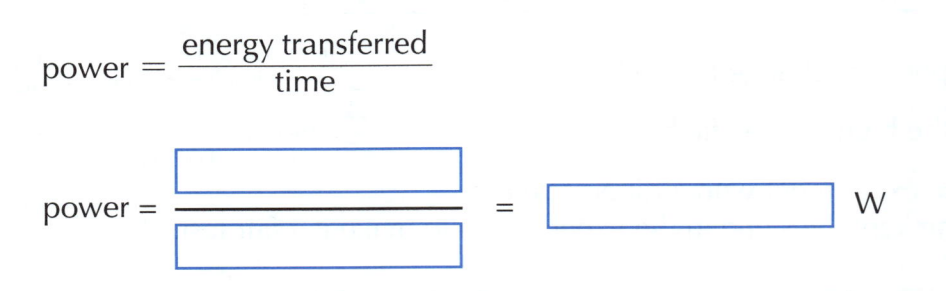

$$\text{power} = \frac{\text{energy transferred}}{\text{time}}$$

power = ☐ / ☐ = ☐ W

Topic P1 — Energy

Q4 For each sentence below, tick to show whether it is true or false.

	True	False
An efficient device doesn't waste much energy.	☐	☐
Most devices are 100% efficient.	☐	☐
A low efficiency means most energy is transferred to useful energy stores.	☐	☐

Q5 50 000 J of energy is transferred to Fatima's lawn mower. It transfers 25 000 J of this energy usefully. Calculate the efficiency of the lawn mower using the equation below. Give your answer as a decimal.

$$\text{efficiency} = \frac{\text{useful output energy transfer}}{\text{total input energy transfer}}$$

Your answer should be a decimal less than 1. If your answer is bigger than 1, you got your numbers the wrong way round.

Efficiency = ...

NOW TRY THIS

I hope you've got some energy left — you're not quite finished...

Energy is often wasted by being transferred to thermal energy stores. For example, when you're charging your phone it might start to feel hot. That's energy being wasted.

1) A goat needs to be lifted up from a cliff using a machine called a winch. The helicopter has two winches. They both have the same power.

   Winch A is 50% efficient. Winch B is 75% efficient.
   The winches have the same energy supplied to them.

   a) Which winch will transfer more energy to useful energy stores?

   b) Which winch will waste the most energy?

   c) Name an energy store that wasted energy will be transferred to.

   d) Winch B is used. Its efficiency of 75% can be written as 0.75.
      10 000 J of energy is transferred to winch B.
      How much energy does the winch transfer usefully?

   $$\text{useful output energy transfer} = \text{efficiency} \times \text{total input energy transfer}$$

   Use the decimal efficiency (0.75) in the equation.

Topic P1 — Energy

Energy Resources and their Uses

There's lots of energy resources on Earth that we can use. Make sure you know the main ones.

Warm-Up

Here are some energy resources.

the Sun   waves   coal   wind

Which of these energy resources is a fossil fuel? ....

Give one way that this energy resource can be used. ....

Q1 Shade each triangle below that contains a renewable energy resource.

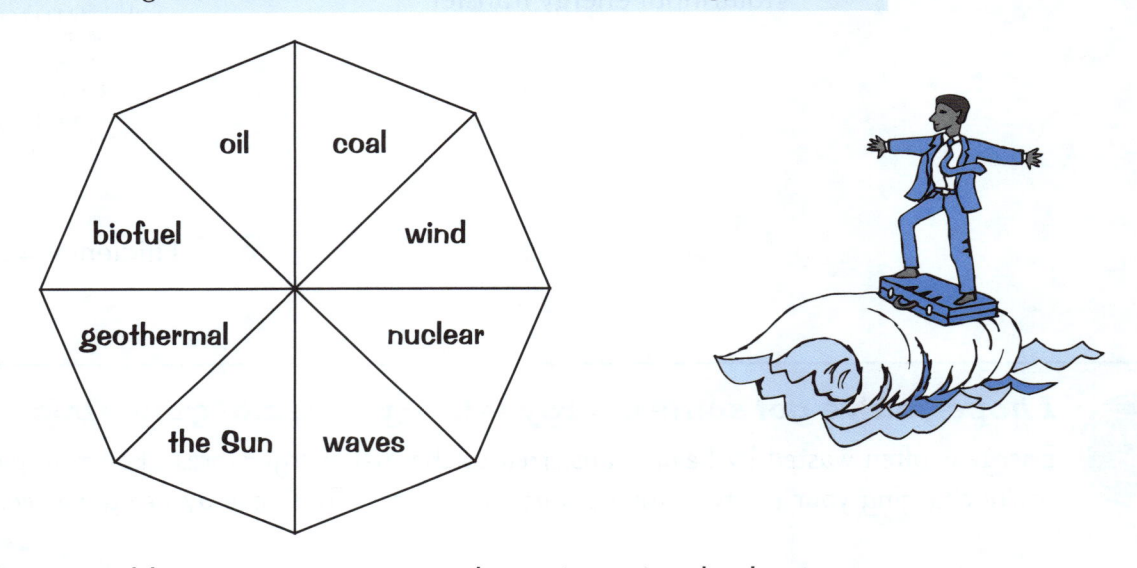

(Octagon divided into 8 triangles labelled: oil, coal, wind, nuclear, waves, the Sun, geothermal, biofuel)

Name a renewable energy resource not shown in a triangle above.

....

Q2 For each sentence below, tick to show whether it is about renewable or non-renewable energy resources.

	Renewable	Non-renewable
This type of energy resource is likely to run out one day.	☐	☐
This type of energy resource can be replaced as it is used.	☐	☐
We cannot replace this type of energy resource as quickly as we are using it.	☐	☐

Topic P1 — Energy

Q3 Energy resources can be used for transport.
Use words from the box to complete the sentences.

| electricity | biofuel | wind | fossil | nuclear |

Most vehicles run on fuel made from oil. Oil is a .... fuel so it will run out one day. Vehicles also run on .... which is a renewable energy resource made from plant products or animal dung. Energy resources are also used to generate .... , which can also be used for transport.

Q4 Circle words in blue to make the sentences correct.

Burning fossil fuels releases **harmful / useful** gases. For example, **oxygen / carbon dioxide** is released. This leads to **global warming / plastic pollution**.

Q5 Why is wind a less reliable energy resource than coal?

....

....

NOW TRY THIS

So many energy resources, so many problems...

All energy resources have their pros and cons. And different people have different views on which we should use more of.

1) Some people are talking about which energy resource they should use to provide their town with electricity. They're choosing between natural gas, hydro-electricity and nuclear fuel.

   a) Give an advantage of choosing a hydro-electric power station.

   b) Give an advantage of choosing a gas-fired power station over a hydro-electric power station.

   c) Suggest one reason why lots of people might not want a nuclear power station.

   d) The Sun rarely shines on this town. However, it is next to the sea. Suggest another energy resource that the town could use to produce electricity.

Choose hydro-electricity.   *A gas-fired power station would be best.*   *Nuclear is the future.*

Topic P1 — Energy

Topic P2 — Electricity

Current and Circuits

Are you feeling electric? Well hopefully by the end of the topic, you'll be one bright spark...

Warm-Up

Name the component shown by each circuit symbol by filling in the missing letters.

A component is just an item in a circuit, like a cell or diode.

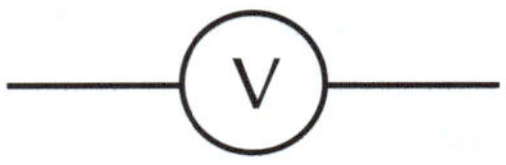

- (V) __olt__e__er 
- (⊗) l__m__ 
- (+ cell) c____l
- (A) ____me__er
- (resistor) r__si____or
- (switch) s__itc__

Q1 Circle the words or phrases in blue to make these sentences correct.

Electric current is the **flow / driving force** of electric charge.

The size of the electric current is the **resistance / rate of flow** of electric charge.

Q2 What do you need for charge to flow through a closed circuit?

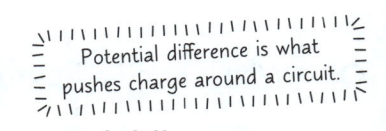

Potential difference is what pushes charge around a circuit.

- ☐ A variable resistor.
- ☐ An open switch.
- ☐ A source of potential difference.
- ☐ A working voltmeter.

Q3 A bulb has a current of 0.3 A through it. How much charge flows through the bulb in 30 seconds? Use the equation below.

charge flow = current × time = ... × .... = ... C

NOW TRY THIS

Electric walk... Electric run... Electric CHARGE...

Well, we never said it was easy — it is physics after all. Get learning as many circuit symbols as you can, because they're going to crop up everywhere in electricity.

1) Adriana sets up the circuit shown on the right.

   a) Name the mystery component.

   b) The current through the mystery component is 0.15 A. How much charge will flow through it in 20 seconds? Use the equation: charge flow = current × time.

   c) What is the size of the current at point X?

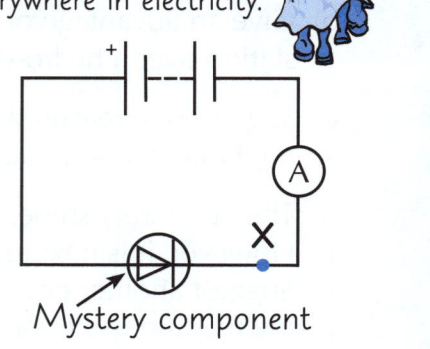

Mystery component

Topic P2 — Electricity

Resistance and I-V Characteristics

The amount of current flowing through something depends on its resistance and potential difference.

Warm-Up

A component has a set potential difference across it. What happens to the size of the current through the component if the resistance is increased?

☐ it increases   ☐ it decreases   ☐ it stays the same

Circle the correct unit for resistance.   amps   ohms   volts   joules

Q1 A current of 0.5 A flows through a 20 Ω resistor. Potential difference, current and resistance are all linked by the equation: potential difference = current × resistance.

Circle the calculation that you would need to do to calculate the potential difference across the resistor.

$$\text{potential difference} = \frac{20}{0.5}$$

$$\text{potential difference} = \frac{0.5}{20}$$

$$\text{potential difference} = 0.5 \times 20$$

Calculate the potential difference across the 20 Ω resistor.

potential difference = ... V

Q2 Three I-V characteristics are shown below. Draw lines to match each device to the correct graph.

An 'I-V characteristic' is a graph showing how the current (I) flowing through a component changes as the potential difference (V) across it changes.

filament lamp   diode   ohmic conductor

Graph A 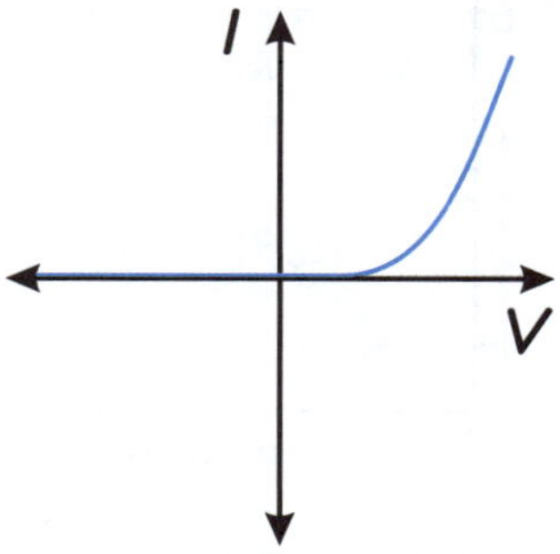   Graph B 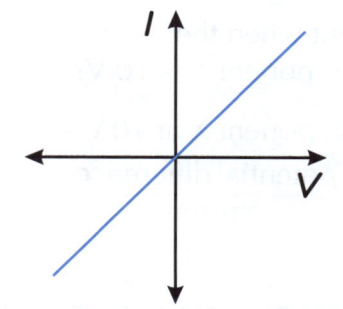   Graph C

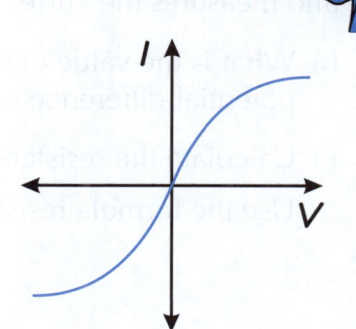

Topic P2 — Electricity

Q3 Circle true or false for the following statements about diodes.

Current can only flow through a diode in one direction. True   False

The resistance of a diode is always the same. True   False

Q4 Choose words from the box to fill in the gaps in the passage about filament lamps.

| increase | decrease | current | resistance |

Increasing the current through a filament lamp causes the

temperature of the filament to ....

This makes the .... of the filament increase.

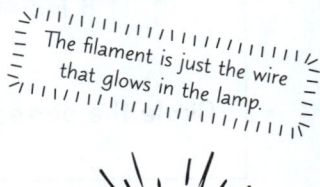

The filament is just the wire that glows in the lamp.

Q5 A wire has a potential difference of 12 V across it and a current of 3 A flowing through it. Calculate the resistance of the wire.

$$\text{resistance} = \frac{\text{potential difference}}{\text{current}}$$

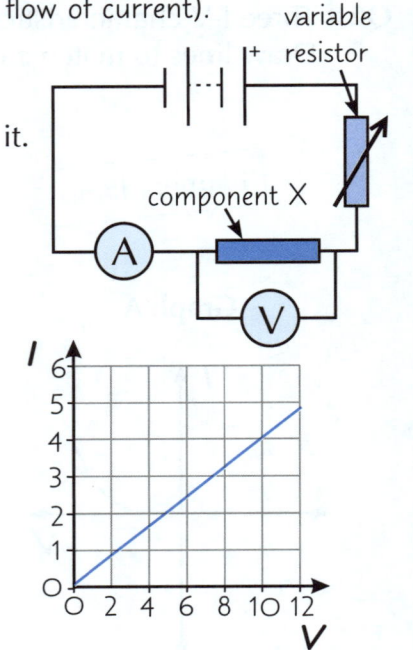

resistance = ... Ω

Don't resist this — use your potential to make a difference...

NOW TRY THIS

Resistance does just what it sounds like it does — it resists (the flow of current).

1) Novak sets up the circuit shown to measure the potential difference across component X and the current flowing through it.

   a) Which component in the circuit can Novak use to change the potential difference across component X?

Novak varies the potential difference across component X and measures the current. His results are shown on the graph:

   b) What is the value of the current when the potential difference across component X is 10 V?

   c) Calculate the resistance of component X at 10 V.
      Use the formula $\text{resistance} = \frac{\text{potential difference}}{\text{current}}$.

Topic P2 — Electricity

Series and Parallel Circuits

The components in series circuits are all connected in a line between the ends of the power supply. In parallel circuits, each component is separately connected to the ends of the power supply.

Warm-Up

Circle the circuit that has all its components connected in series.

Q1 Complete the blue component symbols to show the correct position of the voltmeter and the ammeter.

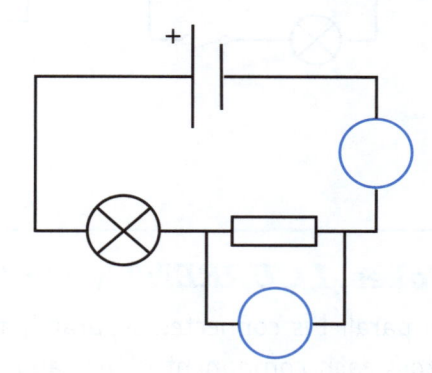

Q2 Circle the equation that would give the total resistance, R_{total}, of the series circuit below.

$R_{total} = \dfrac{1}{3} + \dfrac{1}{4}$

$R_{total} = 3 + 4$

$R_{total} = 3 \times 4$

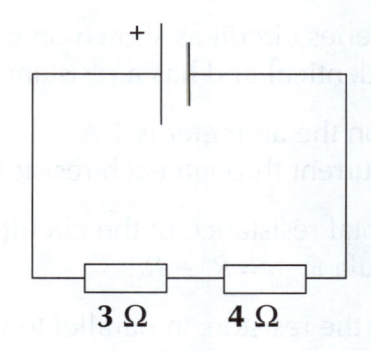

Calculate the resistance of the circuit.

$R_{total} = $ .... Ω

Sherlock Ohms

Topic P2 — Electricity

Q3 A circuit is made up of components connected in parallel with a power supply. Which of the following are true?

☐ The same size current flows through each component.

☐ The potential difference of the power supply is split across the components.

☐ The potential difference across each component is the same.

☐ The total current through the circuit is the sum of the currents through the components.

Q4 In which one of these circuits is there a current flowing? Circle the correct answer.

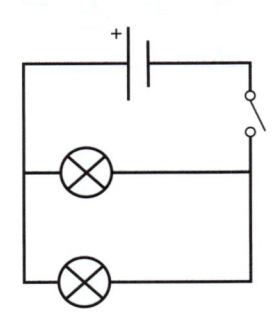

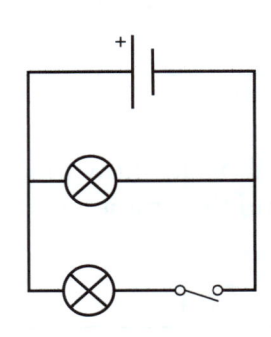

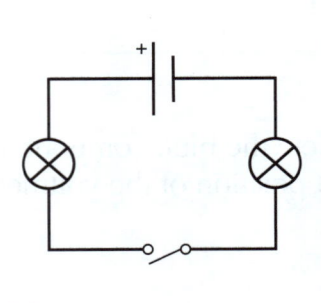

After a series of bad jokes, I CURRENTly can't think of one...

NOW TRY THIS

Each component connected in parallel is connected separately to the ends of the power supply. So the potential difference across each component is the same as that of the power supply.

1) Erica does an experiment to see how the total resistance of a circuit depends on how the resistors in the circuit are connected.

   She sets up the series circuit as shown on the right.
   Each resistor is identical and has a resistance of 3 Ω.

   a) The reading on the ammeter is 1 A.
      What is the current through each resistor?

   b) What is the total resistance of the circuit?
      Use the formula $R_{total} = R_1 + R_2$.

   Erica reconnects the resistors in parallel to make the circuit on the right.
   She says, "The series circuit and the parallel circuit both have the same number of resistors. This means their total resistance will be the same.".

   c) Do you agree? Give a reason for your answer.

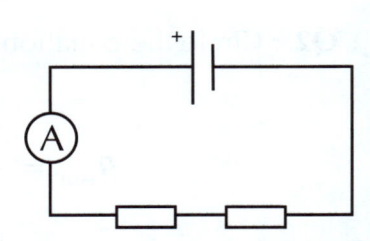

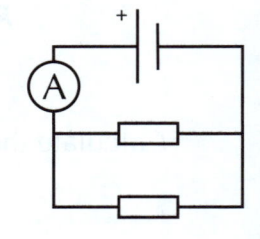

Topic P2 — Electricity

Electricity and Power in the Home

Electrical appliances are just devices that use electricity. They're super useful — where would we be without our TVs and toasters? Bored and with raw toast, I suppose...

Warm-Up

Circle the words in black that make these sentences correct.

The power of an appliance is the **energy** / current it transfers per second.

Alternating current / direct current is a current that constantly reverses direction.

Q1 Use the words from the box to fill in the gaps below.

| power | charge | energy |

Work is done when a ....**charge**........ flows round a circuit.

Whenever work is done, ...**energy**........ is transferred.

The amount of energy transferred by an appliance depends on

the ....**power**........ of the appliance and how long it is switched on for.

Q2 Circle all the boxes that describe the UK mains electricity supply.

50 Hz   alternating current   10 000 V

230 Hz   230 V   direct current

(Circled: 50 Hz, alternating current, 230 V)

Q3 Draw lines to match each type of wire to its colour and its purpose in electrical appliances.

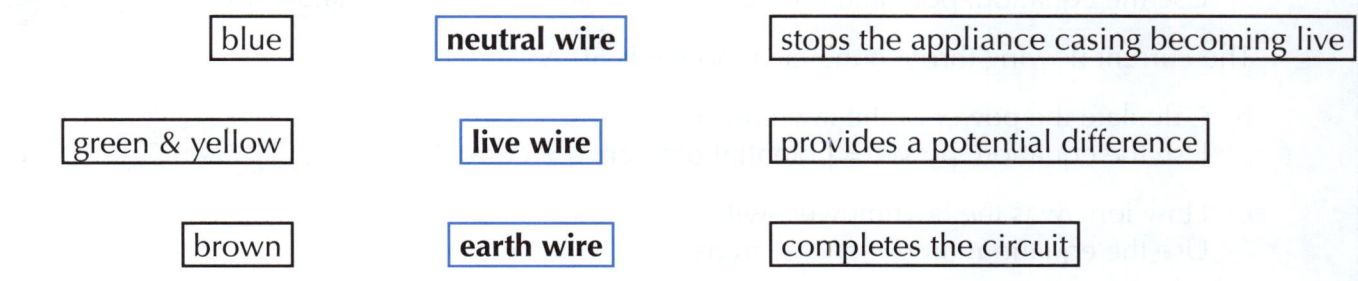

blue	neutral wire	stops the appliance casing becoming live
green & yellow	live wire	provides a potential difference
brown	earth wire	completes the circuit

Topic P2 — Electricity

Q4 The power ratings for three electrical appliances are shown below.

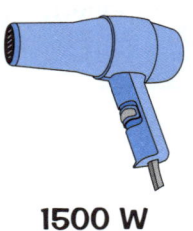

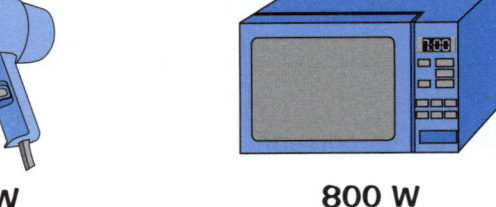

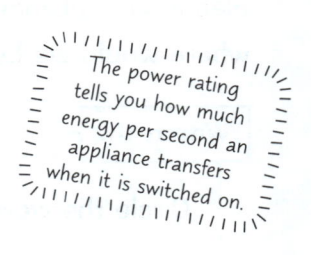

1500 W   **800 W** 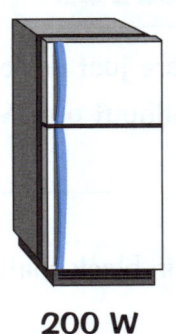   **200 W**

The power rating tells you how much energy per second an appliance transfers when it is switched on.

Each appliance is turned on for 15 seconds. Which appliance will transfer the most energy in that time? Circle the correct appliance above.

Calculate the amount of energy transferred by the microwave in 15 seconds.
Use the equation: energy transferred = power × time

energy transferred = power × time = ... × .... = ... J

Q5 An electric kettle has a power of 1840 W.
The potential difference of the power supply is 230 V.
Calculate the current flowing through the kettle using the equation below.

current = $\dfrac{\text{power}}{\text{potential difference}}$ = $\dfrac{}{}$ = $\boxed{}$ A

Hopefully this hasn't all been too shocking...

NOW TRY THIS

Electricity is so useful, but it can be incredibly dangerous too. Remember, even if an appliance is switched off but plugged in, touching the live wire is still dangerous.

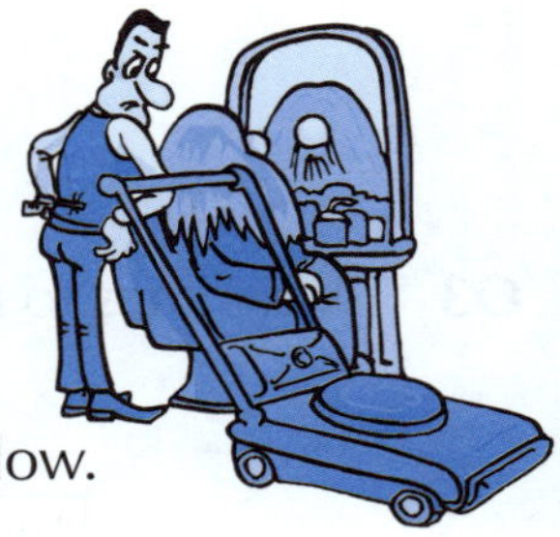

1) Barry has a new battery-powered lawnmower.
   The energy transferred when he uses the lawnmower is 36 000 J.
   The amount of charge that flows through the lawnmower is 3000 C.

   a) Calculate the potential difference of the lawnmower's battery.
      Use the equation: potential difference = energy transferred ÷ charge flow.

   The current flowing through the lawnmower is 50 A.

   b) Calculate the power of the lawnmower.
      Use the equation: power = potential difference × current.

   c) How long was the lawnmower switched on for?
      Use the equation: time = energy transferred ÷ power.

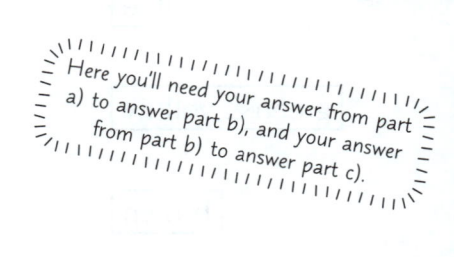

Here you'll need your answer from part a) to answer part b), and your answer from part b) to answer part c).

Topic P2 — Electricity

The National Grid

Electricity has got to get to us somehow — that's where the national grid comes in.

Warm-Up

Which one of these sentences about the national grid is true?

☐ The national grid transfers electrical power from consumers to power stations.

☐ The national grid is a system of cables and transformers.

☐ The national grid only transfers electricity in the daytime.

Consumers means anyone that is using electricity.

Q1 Transformers are devices used in the national grid. Circle the words in blue to make these sentences correct.

Step-up transformers are used to **increase / decrease** potential difference in the national grid. Step-down transformers are used to **increase / decrease** potential difference in the national grid.

Q2 Number the boxes from 1 to 5 to show the journey of electricity through the national grid. Two have been done for you.

☐ step-up transformers   ☐ consumers   [1] power stations

[3] cables   ☐ step-down transformers

I used to think I was a transformer — but then I changed...

Make sure you get your head around what each bit of the national grid is for.

1) Electric current flows across huge distances through large cables in the national grid.

   a) Is a large current or a small current used?

   b) Explain how this helps reduce the amount of energy wasted when current flows through the cables.

   The potential difference of the electricity supplied to UK homes is 230 V. The potential difference across the cables is much higher than this.

   c) What device is used to decrease the potential difference of the electricity supply before it reaches a home?

Topic P2 — Electricity

Topic P3 — Particle Model of Matter

The Particle Model and Density

Models in science aim to show things in a simple way, so they're easier to understand. That's what the balls in boxes coming up on this page are — models showing you the arrangement of particles.

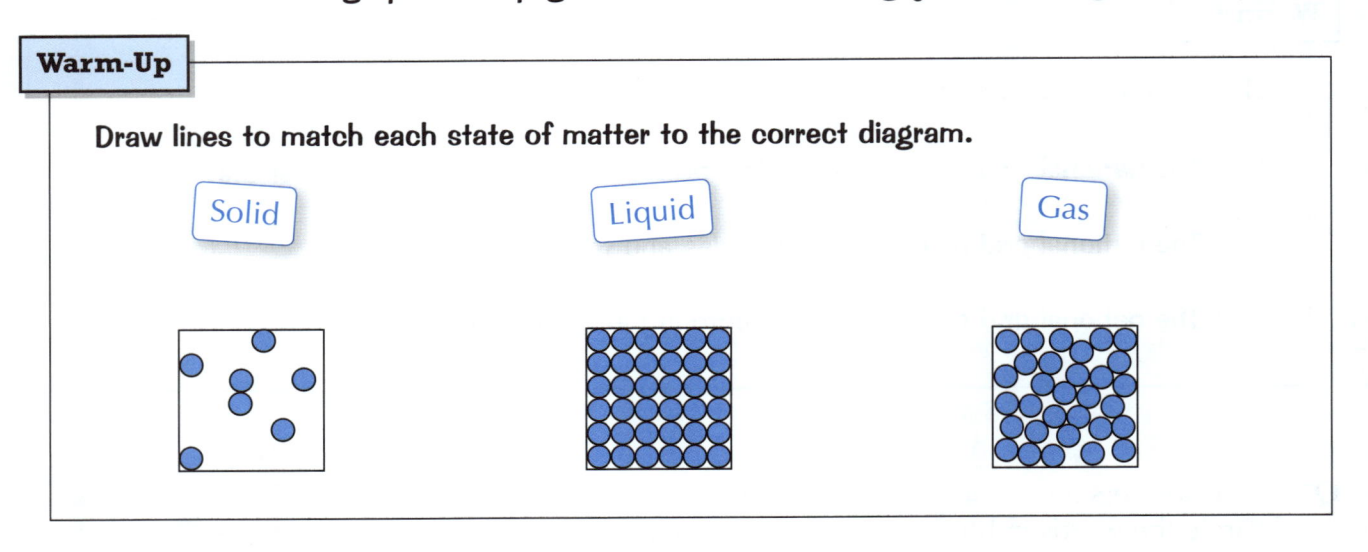

Warm-Up

Draw lines to match each state of matter to the correct diagram.

Solid   Liquid   Gas

Q1 Which state of matter has particles in a fixed, regular pattern?

☐ solid   ☐ liquid   ☐ gas

Q2 Circle blue words to make these sentences correct.

When a material is solid, its particles have **more / less** energy than when the material is a liquid.

The particles in a liquid are close together but **can / can't** move past each other.

The particles in a gas are **close together / far apart** .

Q3 The boxes below contain the same type of particles and all have the same volume. Circle the box with the lowest density.

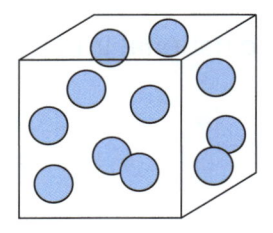

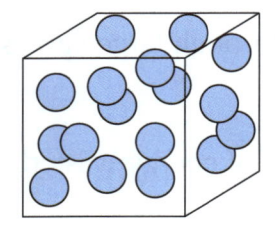

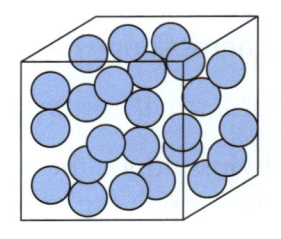

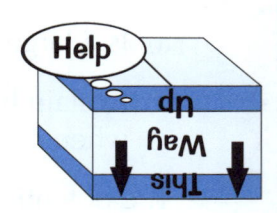

Help: This way up

Explain your answer.

....

....

Q4 A copper block has a mass of 9 kg and a volume of 0.001 m³. Calculate the copper block's density using the equation below.

$$\text{density} = \frac{\text{mass}}{\text{volume}} = \frac{\boxed{}}{\boxed{}} = \boxed{} \text{ kg/m}^3$$

Q5 Solid gold has a density of 19 000 kg/m³ and liquid gold has a density of 17 000 kg/m³. Decide whether the following statements are true or false.

	True	False
The mass of a gold particle is the same in solid gold as in liquid gold.	☐	☐
Solid gold is less dense than liquid gold.	☐	☐
The particles in solid gold are packed more tightly together than the particles in liquid gold.	☐	☐

NOW TRY THIS

The particle model — she looked amazing on the particle catwalk...

You need to know a cunning experiment to find the density of irregularly-shaped objects, such as brass trophies, metal pencil sharpeners... and crowns.

1) Liz wants to find the density of her favourite crown. It has a mass of 0.5 kg.

   She fills a eureka can (a can with a spout in its side) with water and places a measuring cylinder under the spout. She then drops the crown into the water.

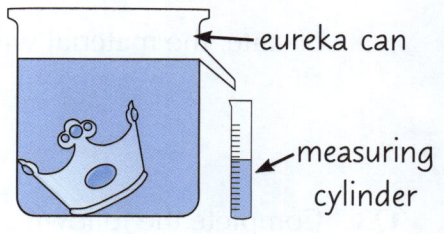

   25 cm³ of water pours out of the eureka can and is collected by the measuring cylinder.

   Remember 1 cm³ = 0.000001 m³

   a) What is the volume of water collected by the measuring cylinder in m³?

   b) What is the volume of the crown in m³?

   c) Calculate the density of the crown using this equation: $\text{density} = \frac{\text{mass}}{\text{volume}}$

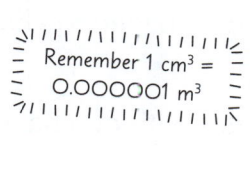

Topic P3 — Particle Model of Matter

Internal Energy, Changes of State and Specific Latent Heat

Solid → Liquid. Liquid → Gas. Texas → California. All of these are changes of state...

Warm-Up

Which of these things stays the same when a substance changes state?

☐ particle arrangement   ☐ mass   ☐ density

Q1 Use the letters on the right to complete the names of the changes of state.

Liquid to gas. b__il__ng

Liquid to solid. f__ee__ing

Gas to liquid. co__de__sa__ion

Solid to gas. su__li__atio__

Q2 Complete the following sentences by using some of the words in the boxes below.

physical   chemical   force   properties

A change of state is a .... change. So if you reverse a change of state, the material will get back all of the .... it once had.

Q3 Complete the following sentence. Specific latent heat of fusion is the amount of energy needed to change 1 kg of a substance...

☐ ...from liquid to gas with no change in temperature.

☐ ...from solid to liquid with no change in temperature.

☐ ...by a temperature of 1 °C.

Topic P3 — Particle Model of Matter

Q4 What is meant by the internal energy of a system?

....

....

Q5 The specific latent heat of vaporisation for mercury is 300 000 J/kg. How much energy is needed to boil 5 kg of liquid mercury to mercury gas at its boiling point? Use the equation below.

energy for a change of state = mass × specific latent heat

= .... × ....

= .... J

Q6 Kevin the scientist says:

> Heating a substance always raises its temperature.

Is he right? Explain your answer.

....

....

....

NOW TRY THIS

All those questions made me a bit hot under the collar...

So many big words... I bet your brain needs a lie down. You can let it do that... or you can have a go at applying your knowledge to the graph question below.

1) A solid lump of metal is heated until it turns into a gas. How the metal's temperature changes is shown below.

   a) Between what temperatures is the metal a liquid?

   b) Explain what happens to the metal between 10 and 20 seconds.

   c) What happens to the temperature of the metal between 30 and 70 seconds?

   d) What is the melting point of the metal?

   e) What is the boiling point of the metal?

   f) After 70 seconds, what is the state of matter (solid, liquid or gas) of the metal?

Topic P3 — Particle Model of Matter

The Current Model of the Atom and Isotopes

Atoms are very small, so let's hope they don't want to go on any roller coasters...

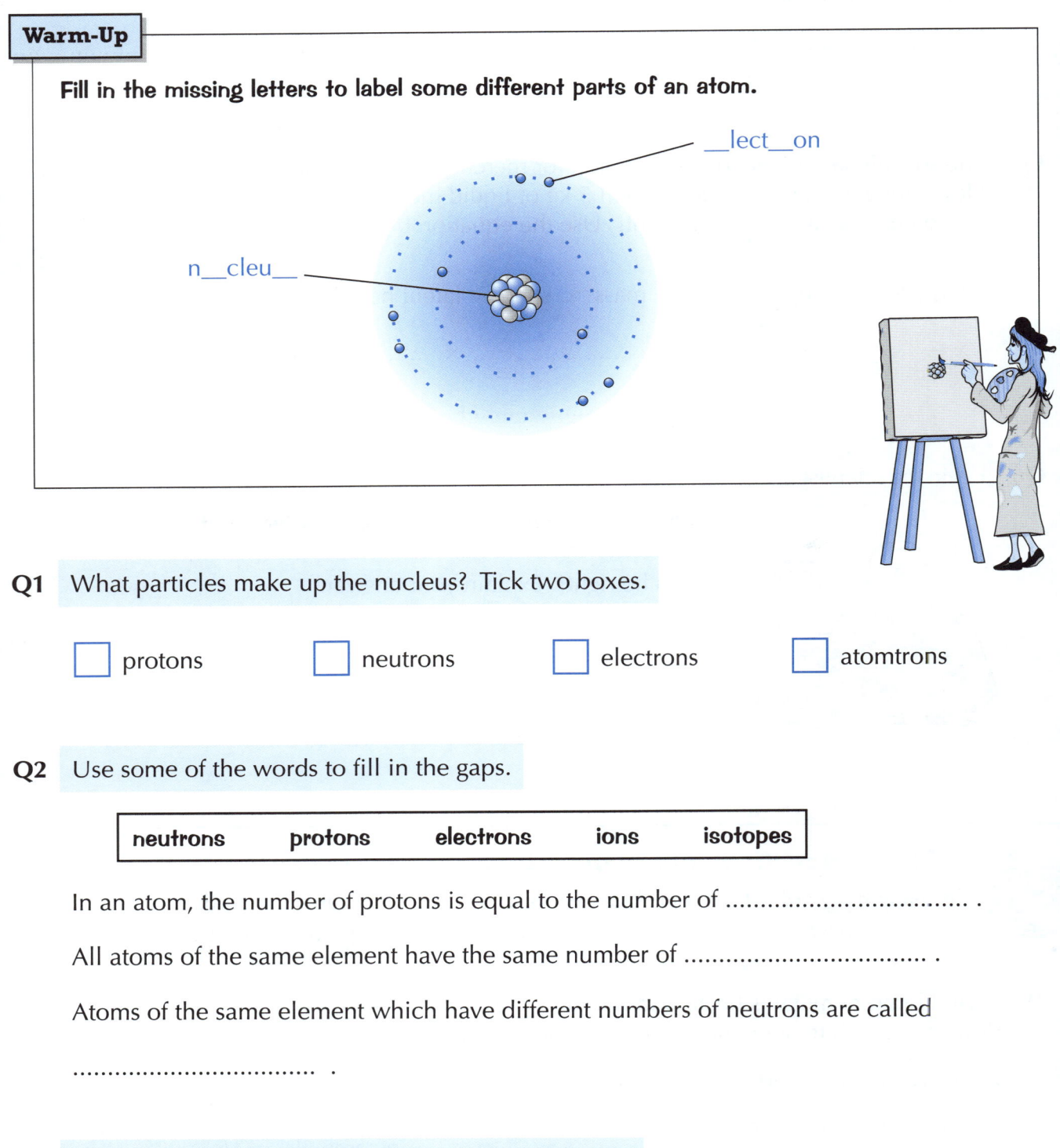

Warm-Up

Fill in the missing letters to label some different parts of an atom.

__lect__on

n__cleu__

Q1 What particles make up the nucleus? Tick two boxes.

☐ protons ☐ neutrons ☐ electrons ☐ atomtrons

Q2 Use some of the words to fill in the gaps.

| neutrons | protons | electrons | ions | isotopes |

In an atom, the number of protons is equal to the number of ....

All atoms of the same element have the same number of ....

Atoms of the same element which have different numbers of neutrons are called

....

Q3 Circle words in blue to make this paragraph correct.

Electrons are arranged in energy levels. Higher energy levels are **closer to / further from** the nucleus. An electron can move to a higher energy level by **absorbing / emitting** electromagnetic radiation. An electron can move to a lower energy level by **absorbing / emitting** electromagnetic radiation.

Emitting radiation just means releasing radiation.

Topic P4 — Atomic Structure

Q4 Fill in the crossword using the clues. One has been done for you.

The numbers at the end of each clue tell you how many letters are in each word of the answer.

Across

2) Atoms have no overall _____ . (6)

4) This is the sum of the number of protons and neutrons. (4, 6)

7) Atoms turn into positive ions if they lose one or more of these. (9)

Down

1) Electrons move around the nucleus in these. (6, 6)

3) This is the type of charge on an electron. (8)

5) This is where most of the mass of an atom is. (7)

6) The atomic number tells you how many of these there are. (7)

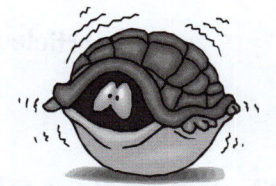

Judy's best neutron impression

Neutrons don't need to carry money — they are never charged...

Only a tiny bit of an atom is filled with protons, neutrons and electrons. The rest of the atom is empty — a bit like the beach on a rainy Tuesday in November.

1) The table shows the number of protons, neutrons and electrons for some isotopes.

	Hydrogen	Deuterium	Tritium
protons	1	1	1
neutrons	0	1	2
electrons	1	1	1

a) What is the atomic number of deuterium?

b) What is the mass number of tritium?

c) Explain why an atom of hydrogen has no overall charge.

d) Explain why hydrogen, deuterium and tritium are isotopes of each other.

A hydrogen atom absorbs electromagnetic radiation. It loses its electron and becomes an ion.

e) Is the charge on the hydrogen ion positive or negative?

Topic P4 — Atomic Structure

Radioactive Decay and Properties of Nuclear Radiation

Nuclear radiation won't turn you into a superhero, but it might help stabilise an isotope...

Warm-Up

Choose from the words shown to complete the sentences:

Unstable isotopes are ....

They give out nuclear radiation to become more ....

This process is called radioactive ....

Words: decay, radioactive, stable

Q1 Which one of these is **not** a type of nuclear radiation? Circle your answer.

alpha particles   beta particles   becquerels   neutrons

Q2 Which of the following makes up an alpha particle?

☐ 40 neutrons and 80 protons

☐ 2 neutrons and 2 protons

☐ 2 neutrons, 2 protons and 2 fast-moving electrons

Alpha Particle... Reveal yourself!

Q3 Draw lines to match each type of radiation to its symbol **and** its description.

alpha particles	γ	high speed electron
beta particles	α	electromagnetic wave
gamma rays	β	helium nucleus

Q4 In a radioactive atom, a neutron turns into a proton and radiation is given out. State the type of radiation this is.

....

Topic P4 — Atomic Structure

Q5 For each fact below, tick whether it is true for alpha, beta or gamma radiation.

	alpha	beta	gamma
It is strongly ionising.	☐	☐	☐
It has the weakest ionising power of the three.	☐	☐	☐
It has a range in air of a few metres.	☐	☐	☐
It can be stopped by a sheet of paper.	☐	☐	☐

Q6 What is meant by ionising power?

☐ How easily radiation can knock neutrons out of nuclei.

☐ The energy transferred per second by an ion.

☐ How easily radiation can knock electrons off atoms.

☐ How long it takes an unstable atom to decay.

I have the power.

NOW TRY THIS

Radioactive decay — not as stinky as it sounds...

Alpha, beta and gamma are all types of nuclear radiation — but you'll know that by now. However, *did you know* that it's impossible to hum while you hold your nose?

1) Mohammed has three radioactive sources — X, Y and Z. One source emits alpha radiation, one emits beta radiation and one emits gamma radiation.

   He places each source in turn in front of a detector. A sheet of aluminium is placed in front of the source, as shown.

   a) Only the radiation from source X reaches the detector. What type of radiation does source X give out? Explain how you know this.

   The sheet of aluminium is removed and each source is placed in turn 1 m away from the detector.

   b) The radiation from source Y doesn't reach the detector. What type of radiation does source Y give off? Explain how you know.

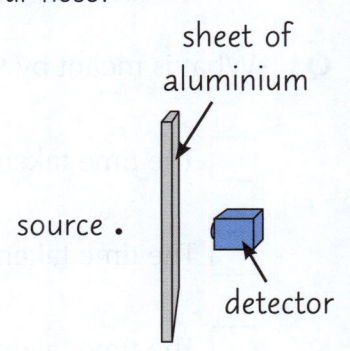

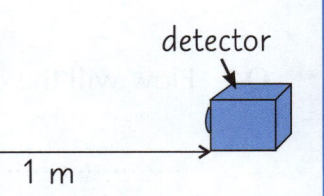

Topic P4 — Atomic Structure

Half-life

If you like third-life or quarter-life, then these pages are going to be a bit of a disappointment. But if you like half-life you're going to absolutely love them.

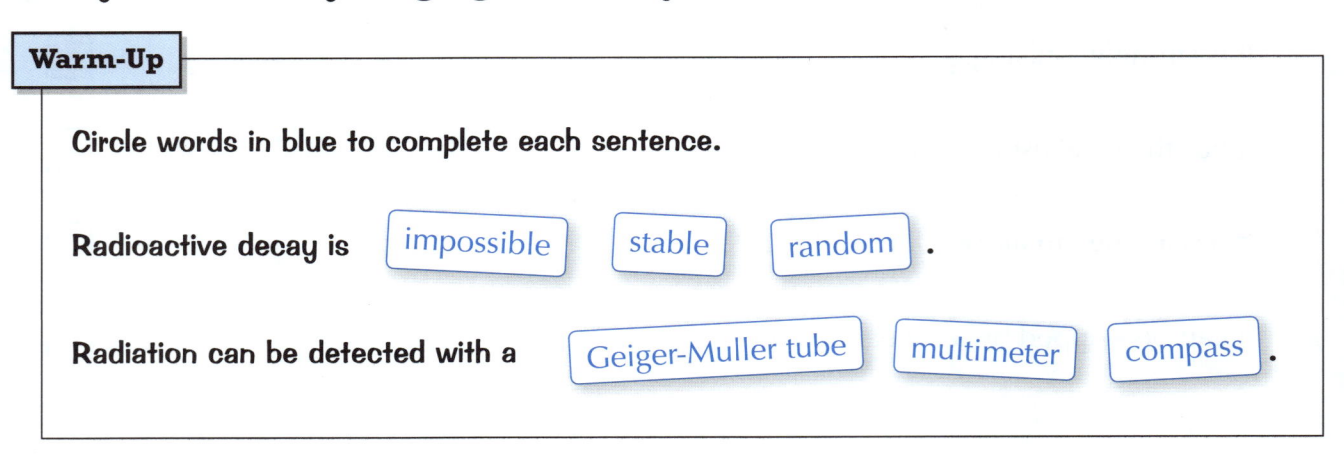

Warm-Up

Circle words in blue to complete each sentence.

Radioactive decay is   impossible   stable   random .

Radiation can be detected with a   Geiger-Muller tube   multimeter   compass .

Q1 Circle words in blue to make these sentences correct.

The rate at which a radioactive source decays is called its **activity / half-life** . The number of radioactive decays recorded each second by a detector is called the **nuclear rate / count-rate** .

Q2 What is the rate of radioactive decay measured in? Circle your answer.

metres   becquerels   seconds   volts

Q3 What is meant by the half-life of a radioactive sample?

☐ The time taken for the sample to split in half.

☐ The time taken for the sample to stop being radioactive.

☐ The time taken for the number of nuclei of the radioactive isotope in the sample to halve.

Q4 How will the count-rate from a radioactive sample have changed after one half-life?

....

Topic P4 — Atomic Structure

Q5 Which of the following can you predict about a decaying radioactive sample?

☐ The nucleus in the sample that will decay next.

☐ The time it will take for half of the nuclei to decay.

☐ How to stop the sample from decaying.

Radioactivity = tunes

Q6 The activity of a radioactive sample takes 6 seconds to fall from 6000 Bq to 3000 Bq. How long will it take the activity of the radioactive sample to fall from 3000 Bq to 1500 Bq?

....

Q7 The initial activity of a sample of a radioactive isotope is 1000 Bq. The half-life of the sample is 10 seconds. What will the activity of the sample be after 10 seconds?

The initial activity just means the activity it starts with.

☐ 500 Bq   ☐ 100 Bq   ☐ 250 Bq   ☐ 1000 Bq

What will the activity of the sample be after 20 seconds?

....

Here's an activity — learning about the rate of radioactive decay...

NOW TRY THIS

The half-life of a radioactive sample can be really big or really small. If it's really big (like a billion years) then you've probably got time to make a cuppa before the next nucleus decays...

1) A scientist is investigating a sample of radioactive carbon-10.

The activity of the sample of carbon-10 decreases with time, as shown on the graph to the right.

a) What is the activity of the sample when the time is at 0 s?

b) How many seconds does it take for the activity to halve?

c) What is the half-life of carbon-10?

d) How many half-lives have passed when the activity has fallen to 300 Bq?

Count how many times you have to halve the activity to get to 300 Bq.

Topic P4 — Atomic Structure

Forces, Resultant Forces and Work Done

A force is a push or pull that acts on an object. Contact forces act on objects that are touching. Non-contact forces act on objects that aren't touching. There's lots more on forces to come...

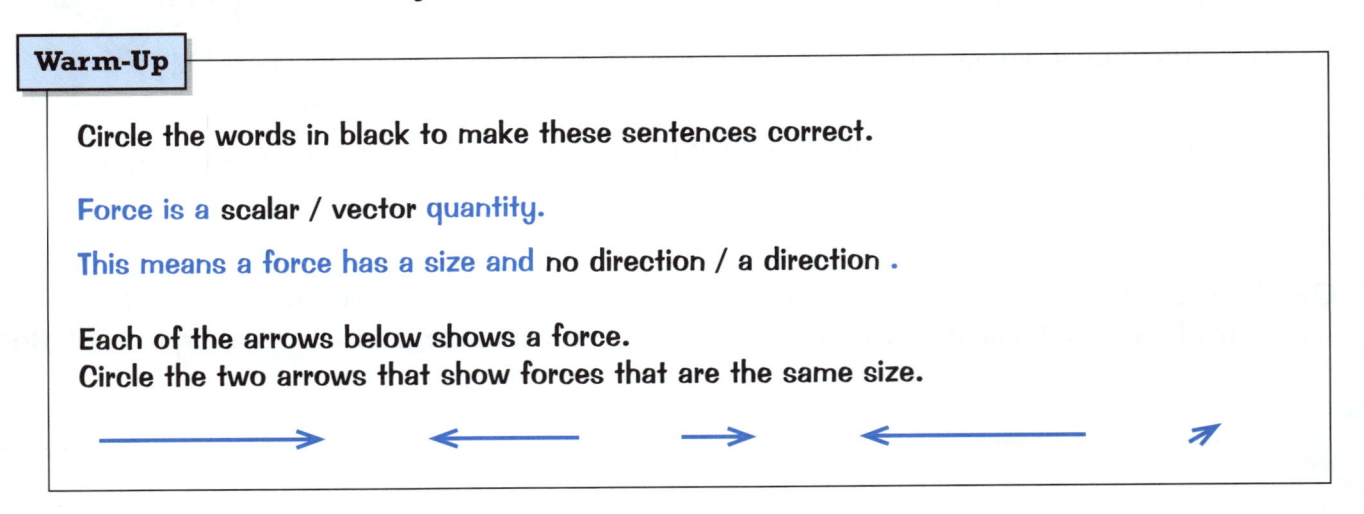

Warm-Up

Circle the words in black to make these sentences correct.

Force is a scalar / **vector** quantity.

This means a force has a size and no direction / **a direction**.

Each of the arrows below shows a force.
Circle the two arrows that show forces that are the same size.

⟶   ⟵   →   ⟵   ↗

Q1 Cross out all of the non-contact forces below. The first one has been done for you.

~~magnetic force~~   friction   gravitational force   normal contact force   electrostatic force

Q2 Several forces act on an object. Arin, Dave and Mia are talking about the resultant force on the object. Who is correct? Circle their name.

- The resultant force is the largest force.
- The resultant force is the smallest force.
- The resultant force is the overall force on the object.

Arin   Dave   Mia

Q3 Decide whether each statement about work done is true or false.

	True	False
Energy is always transferred when work is done.	☐	☐
When a force moves an object, work is always done.	☐	☐
Force and work done can both be measured in newton metres.	☐	☐

Q4 What is the size of the resultant force on each frog?

10 N ← → 8 N

Frog 1

Size of resultant force = ... N

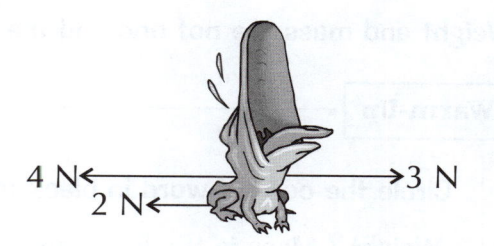

4 N ← → 3 N
2 N ←

Frog 2

Size of resultant force = ... N

Q5 A horizontal force of 5 N pushes a ball along flat ground. The ball travels 18 m. Calculate the work done by the force.

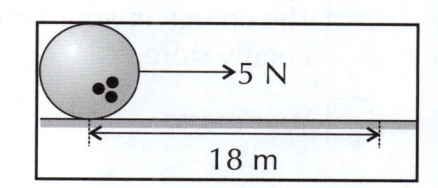

work done = force × distance

= .... × ....

= .... J

Q6 Circle the equation below that you could use to calculate the distance moved by an object from the work done and the force on the object.

distance = force × work done

distance = work done ÷ force

distance = force ÷ work done

You need to put in the work to go the distance...

NOW TRY THIS

Always remember that when a force is moving an object, work is being done. And whenever work is being done, energy is being transferred.

1) Wayne pulls a box 2.5 m across the floor. The resultant force on the box is 50 N.

   50 N ←

   a) How much work is done moving the box? Use the equation: work done = force × distance.

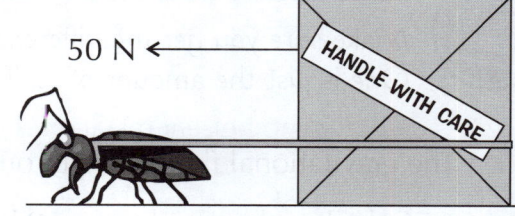

   b) Wayne touches the bottom of the box after he has pulled it. The bottom of the box feels warmer than the rest of the box. Wayne says, 'The increased temperature of the box is due to work being done.' Do you agree? Explain your answer.

Topic P5 — Forces

Weight, Mass and Gravity

Weight and mass are not one and the same, but they are linked — through gravity.

Warm-Up

Circle the correct word in black to complete the sentence.

Weight / Mass is the force on an object due to gravity.

Which of these is a piece of equipment that can be used to measure weight?

☐ ammeter ☐ tape measure ☐ newtonmeter

Q1 What causes you to have weight? Tick two boxes.

☐ The energy in your kinetic energy store.
☐ Your mass.
☐ The Earth's gravitational field.
☐ Friction.

Q2 The gravitational field strength on Earth is 9.8 N/kg.
Calculate the weight of an object on Earth that has a mass of 20 kg.

Weight = mass × gravitational field strength

= .... × .... = ... N

Q3 The gravitational field strength on the Moon is lower than the gravitational field strength on Earth. Circle the correct blue words to complete the following sentences.

Your **weight** on the Moon would be **the same as / less than / more than** your weight on Earth.

Your **mass** on the Moon would be **the same as / less than / more than** your mass on Earth.

NOW TRY THIS

Your brain will feel massive after all this practice...

Make sure you get the difference between mass and weight drilled into your mind. One is just the amount of stuff something is made of, the other is a force.

1) The gravitational field strength on Mars is around 3.7 N/kg.

a) Calculate the weight of a 10 kg rock on Mars.
Use the equation: weight = mass × gravitational field strength.

b) A martian weighs 111 N on Mars. Calculate his mass.
Use the equation: mass = weight ÷ gravitational field strength.

Topic P5 — Forces

Forces and Elasticity

Applying forces to things can streeeeeeeeeeeeeeeeetch them out...

> **Warm-Up**
>
> True or false? More than one force needs to act on a still object to change its shape.   ☐ True   ☐ False

Q1 Circle the words in blue to make these sentences correct.

Work is done to stretch a spring. This causes energy to be transferred to the spring's **elastic / gravitational** potential energy store. The spring returns to its original shape after the forces acting on it are removed. This is an example of an **elastic / inelastic** deformation.

'Deformation' just means the spring has changed shape.

Q2 A spring has a spring constant of 2.5 N/m. Calculate the force used to extend this spring by 0.2 m.

'Extend' just means stretch. The spring constant tells you how stiff the spring is.

force = spring constant × extension = ... × .... = ... N

Q3 A spring is stretched elastically. Complete the sentence using one of the phrases on the right.

The work done on the spring is ....

the energy in the elastic potential energy store of the spring.

equal to

less than

greater than

NOW TRY THIS

That was quite a stretch...
Make sure you know the difference between elastic and inelastic deformations, it'll come in handy.

1) Yin hangs a spring from a clamp and attaches a marker to the end of the spring. The spring is 2.6 cm long. She adds a mass to the end of the spring, as shown on the right. The mass causes a force of 0.5 N to act on the spring.

   a) Read off the new length of the spring, shown by the marker in the diagram.

   b) Calculate the extension of the spring in metres.

   c) Calculate the spring constant of the spring in N/m. Use the equation: spring constant = force ÷ extension.

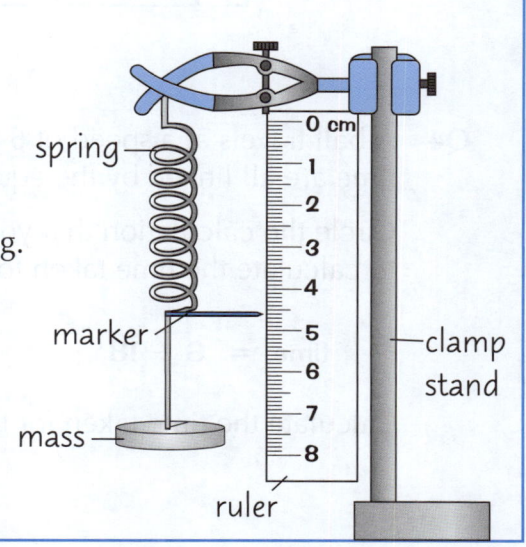

Topic P5 — Forces

Distance, Speed and Acceleration

Speed is just how fast something goes. Acceleration is how quickly something changes velocity.

Warm-Up

Circle all of the vector quantities below.

Distance   Displacement   Velocity   Speed

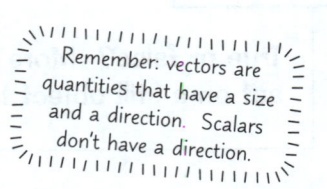

Remember: vectors are quantities that have a size and a direction. Scalars don't have a direction.

Q1 An object moves. What is its displacement?

☐ The distance and direction in a straight line of the object from its starting point.

☐ The distance an object has travelled multiplied by its speed.

☐ The total distance travelled by the object.

Q2 Tick a box to correctly complete the following sentence.
A car that is speeding up is...

☐ accelerating   ☐ decelerating   ☐ not changing velocity

Q3 Draw lines to match each speed to its correct typical value.

A person's walking speed	6 m/s
A person's running speed	1.5 m/s
A person's cycling speed	3 m/s

Q4 A ball travels at a speed of 6 m/s. It travels 18 m. Speed, distance and time are all linked by the equation: time = distance travelled ÷ speed.

Circle the calculation that you would need to do
to calculate the time taken for the ball to travel 18 m.

time = 6 ÷ 18   time = 18 ÷ 6   time = 6 × 18

Calculate the time taken for the ball to travel 18 m.

Time = ... s

Topic P5 — Forces

Q5 Which of the following symbols can be used in an equation to mean 'change in' something? Circle the correct answer.

θ   Δ   Ω   α   β

Q6 What is the acceleration of any object falling freely under gravity near the Earth's surface?

☐ 1.6 m/s²   ☐ 9.8 m/s²   ☐ 15 m/s   ☐ 9.8 m/s

Q7 An object's velocity increases from 20 m/s to 50 m/s in 8 seconds.

What is the object's change in velocity?

Change in velocity = ... m/s

Calculate the average acceleration of the object.

$$\text{average acceleration} = \frac{\text{change in velocity}}{\text{time taken}}$$

Average acceleration = ... m/s²

Time to get yourself up to speed...

Make sure you've got your head around the difference between speed and velocity, and distance and displacement. Think you know your stuff? Try this question out...

1) A crab searches for clams on a beach. The diagram on the right shows the crab's path.

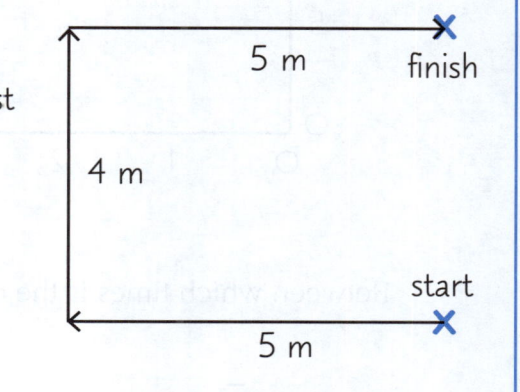

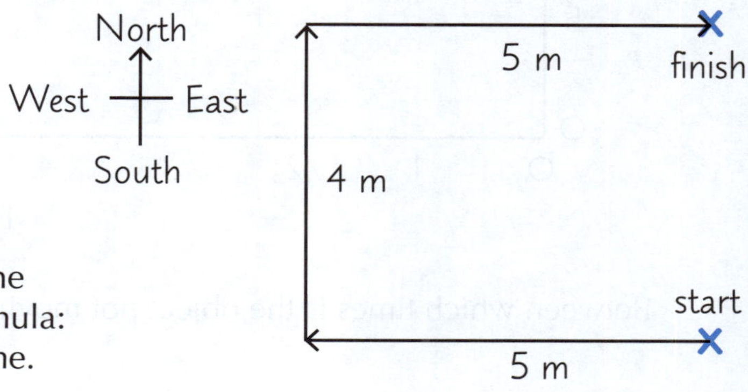

   a) What is the total distance travelled by the crab?

   b) It takes the crab 20 seconds to get from the start to the finish point. Calculate the average speed of the crab. Use the formula: average speed = distance travelled ÷ time.

   c) Which of the following is the crab's final displacement?

   4 m North   5 m East   14 m North   4 m South

Topic P5 — Forces

Distance- and Velocity-Time Graphs

Graphs can look complicated but if you practise using them, you won't lose the plot.

Warm-Up

Draw lines to match each label to the distance-time graph it describes.

- A stationary object
- An object accelerating
- An object moving at a steady speed

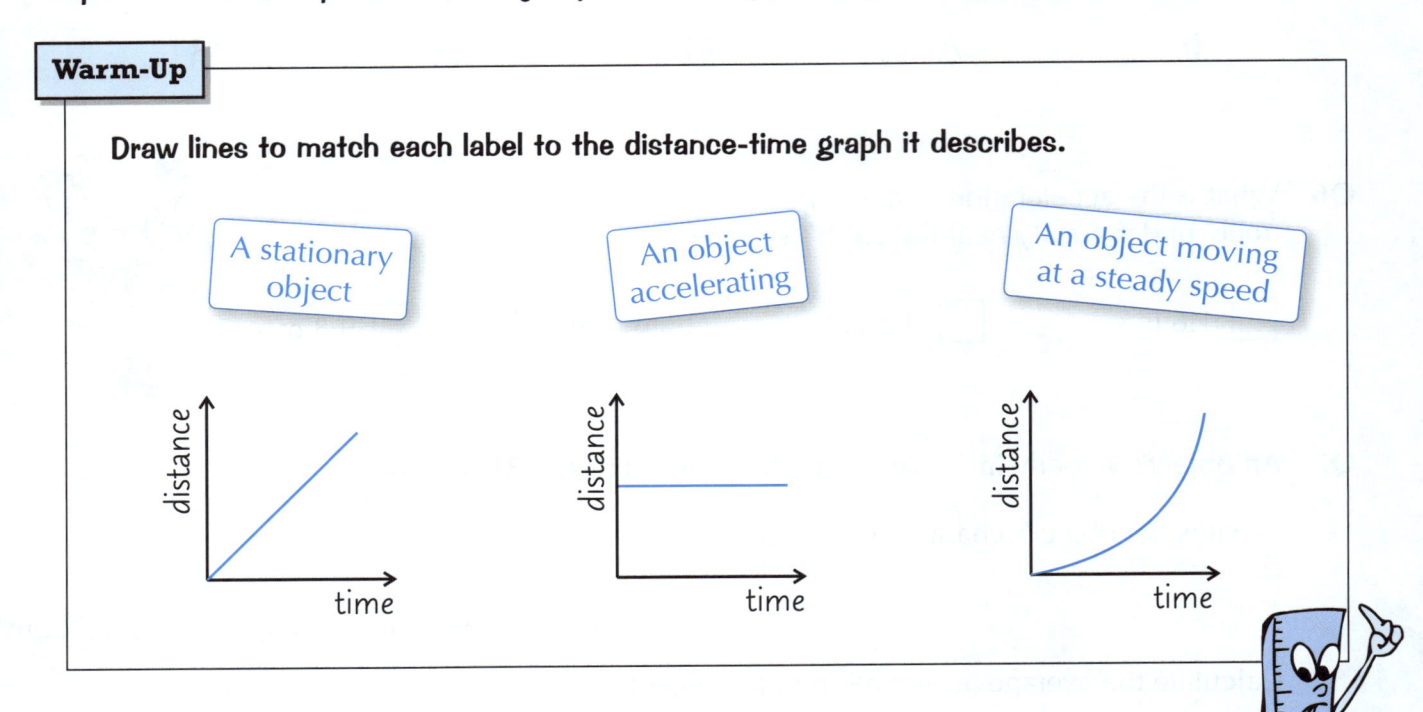

Q1 Plot the points from the table onto the distance-time graph. Join up the points with straight lines.

Always use a ruler to draw straight lines.

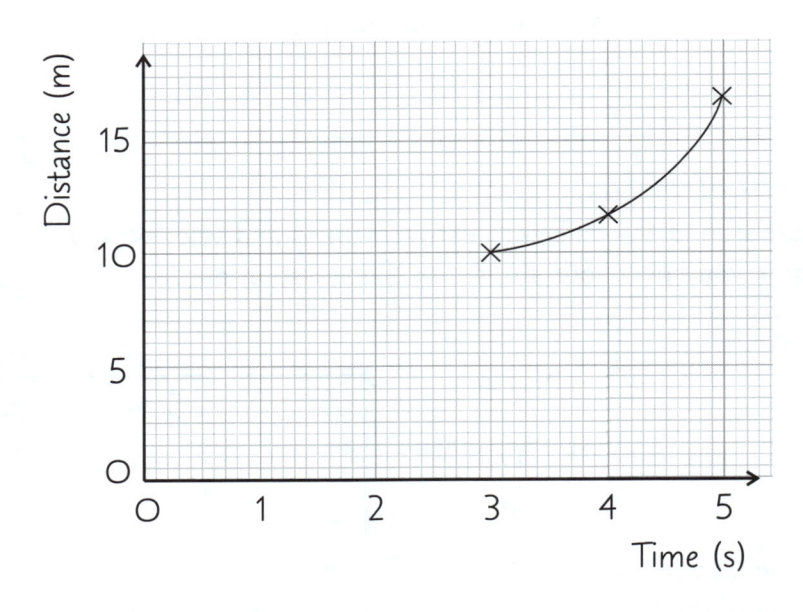

Time (secs)	Distance (m)
0	0
1	5
2	10

Between which times is the object not moving? .... s and .... s

Which of the following is given by the gradient of a distance-time graph?

☐ speed   ☐ acceleration   ☐ distance travelled

Topic P5 — Forces

Q2 Choose from the blue phrases below to fill in the labels on the velocity-time graph.

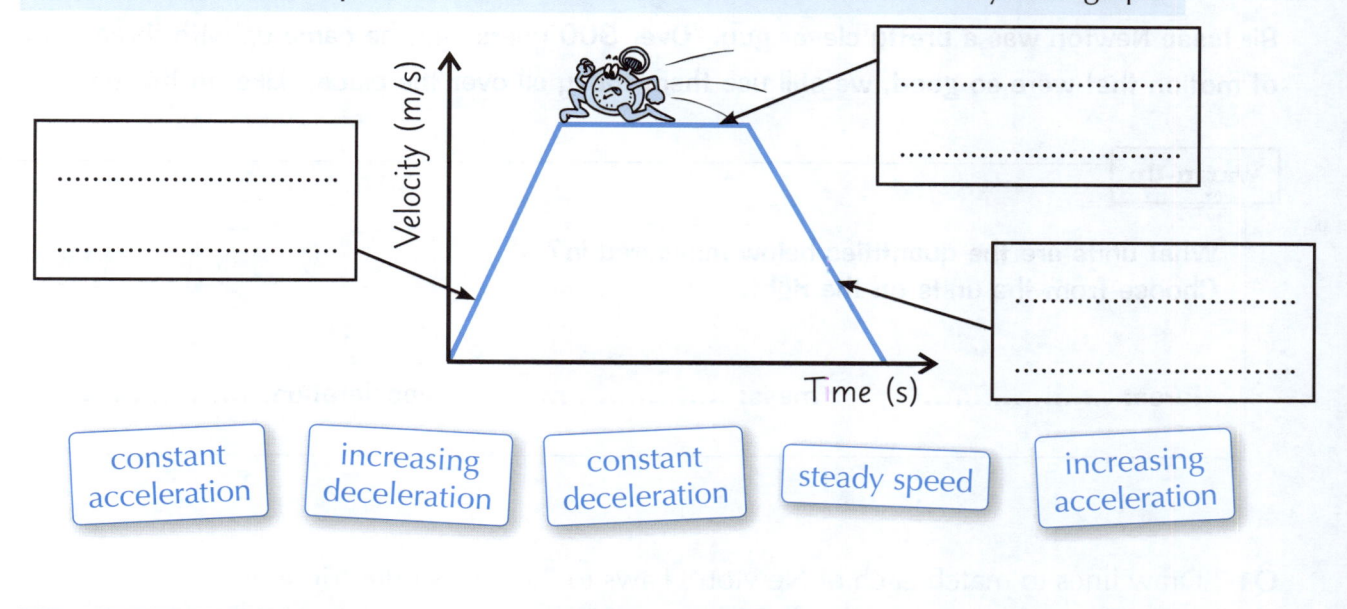

constant acceleration | increasing deceleration | constant deceleration | steady speed | increasing acceleration

Q3 The velocity-time graph shows two objects, A and B, accelerating. Which object has the greatest acceleration?

☐ A ☐ B

Explain why.

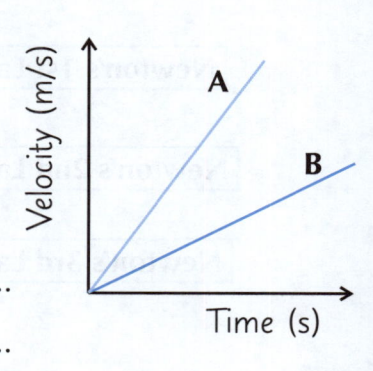

....

....

I like graphs — but after a certain point, you have to draw the line...

NOW TRY THIS

Phew, that was a lot of graphs — here's the last one. Make sure you keep your pencil (and your brain) sharp when you're drawing graphs.

1) The distance-time graph below shows part of Alex's journey to school.

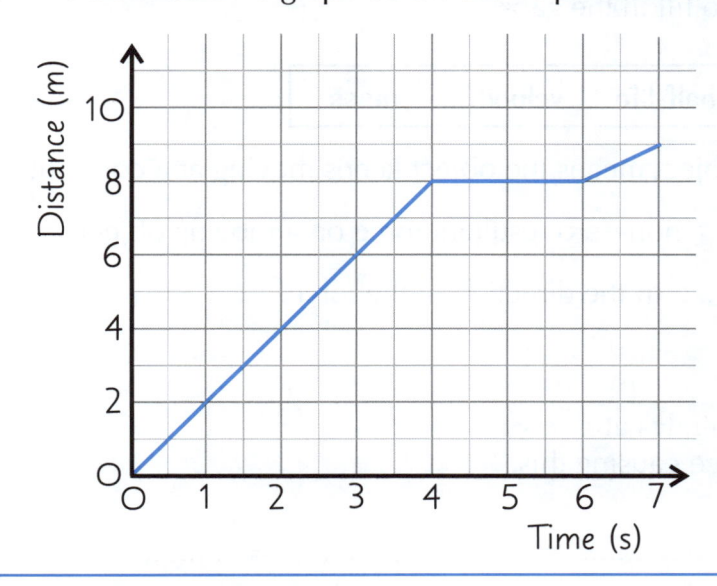

   a) How long does it take Alex to travel the first 6 m?

   b) For how many seconds does she stop moving?

   Speed is given by the gradient of a line on a distance-time graph.

   c) Calculate the speed that Alex travels at for the first 4 seconds of her journey.

   $$\text{Gradient} = \frac{\text{change in vertical axis}}{\text{change in horizontal axis}}$$

Topic P5 — Forces

Newton's Laws

Sir Isaac Newton was a pretty clever guy. Over 300 years ago, he came up with three laws of motion that were so good, we still use them today all over the place. Like on this page.

Warm-Up

What units are the quantities below measured in? Choose from the units on the right.

m/s^2 N   kg

force: ....   mass: ....   acceleration: ....

Q1 Draw lines to match each of Newton's Laws to the correct description.

To exert a force on something just means to apply a force to it.

Newton's 1st Law — The forces two objects exert on each other are equal and opposite.

Newton's 2nd Law — A resultant force is needed to change an object's motion.

Newton's 3rd Law — Resultant force = mass × acceleration

Q2 This apple is stationary — it isn't moving. What is the resultant force on the apple?

....

Q3 Use the correct words from the box to fill in the gaps.

| accelerate | half-life | velocity | mass |

A zero resultant force on a moving object means the object keeps moving at a constant .... If there is a non-zero resultant force on a moving object, the object will .... in the direction of the force.

Q4 An object with a mass of 25 kg accelerates at 4 m/s². Calculate the size of the resultant force causing this.

Force = mass × acceleration = ... × .... = ... N

Topic P5 — Forces

Q5 A girl pushes against a wall with a force of 50 N. How much force does a wall push back with?

☐ 0 N   ☐ 25 N   ☐ 50 N   ☐ 100 N

Which of Newton's Laws is this an example of?

....

Q6 A resultant force of 10 N acts on a 5 kg object. Its acceleration is 2 m/s².

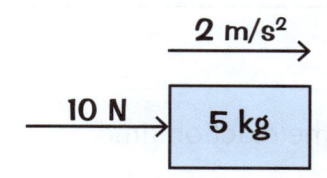

The resultant force on the object doubles to 20 N. What is the object's new acceleration?

☐ 1 m/s²   ☐ 2 m/s²   ☐ 4 m/s²   ☐ 8 m/s²

GCSE Physics might have been a piece of cake if it wasn't for Newton...
Force this forces stuff into your brain — Newton's laws crop up a lot in physics.

1) A trolley and pulley system is set up as shown to measure acceleration. The system includes the trolley, the pulley, the hook and any masses added. Masses are hung from the hook and the acceleration of the system is measured by the light gate as the trolley passes through it.

   a) What makes up the total mass that is being accelerated?

   b) What causes the force that makes the trolley accelerate?

The masses on the hook are kept the same. Masses are added to the top of the trolley one at a time.

   c) The acceleration of the system is measured for different masses. What happens to the acceleration as the mass is increased?

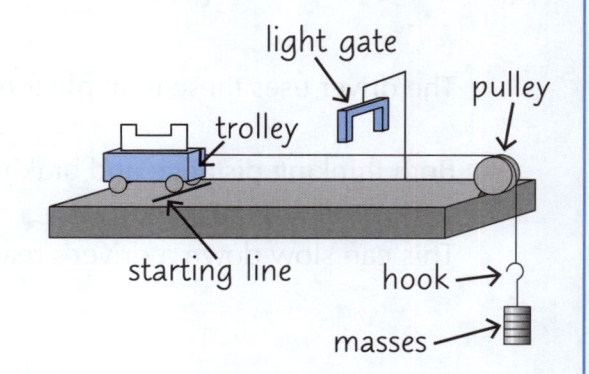

Total mass of the system (kg)	acceleration (m/s²)
0.2	5
0.3	3.3
0.4	2.5
0.5	2

Topic P5 — Forces

Stopping Distances and Reaction Times

Reaction times are just one of the things that can affect how quickly a vehicle comes to a stop. And if there's a hazard in the road, it's very important that the vehicle stops in time...

Warm-Up

Put the correct terms into the equation for the distance it takes to stop a vehicle in an emergency.

.... = ... + ...

thinking distance   *stopping distance*   *braking distance*

Q1 True or false? Everyone has the same reaction time.

☐ True   ☐ False

Q2 Which of these is a typical reaction time for a person?

☐ 0.0001 s   ☐ 0.4 s   ☐ 20 s   ☐ 4 years

Q3 Use the clues to figure out the missing letters in the words on the right.

The driver uses these to apply force to stop a vehicle.　　　br____es

Both thinking distance and braking distance are affected by this.　　s____ed

This can slow down a driver's reaction time.　　al____ho__

Q4 Circle words in blue to make these sentences correct.

The distance a car travels during the driver's reaction time is known as the

thinking distance / braking distance. The distance a car travels under the braking force

is known as the **thinking distance / braking distance**. For a given braking force,

the faster the speed of a vehicle, the **larger / smaller** the stopping distance.

Topic P5 — Forces

Q5 Put each factor in the correct column in the table to show whether it affects thinking distance or braking distance.

tiredness, worn brakes, distractions, drugs, worn tyres, icy roads

Thinking distance	Braking distance

Q6 Complete the blanks in the table by calculating the missing distances.

	stopping distance (m)	thinking distance (m)	braking distance (m)
40 mph	36	12	24
50 mph	....	15	38
60 mph	73	....	55

Stop, in the name of safety...

There are lots of different factors that affect stopping distance. And stopping distance is important — it can mean the difference between crashing or not.

1) The bar chart on the right shows typical stopping distances for different speeds of a car.

   Key: braking distance, thinking distance

   a) What is the thinking distance of a car travelling at 40 mph?

   b) How does the speed of the car affect thinking distance?

   c) What is the stopping distance of the car when travelling at 30 mph?

   d) The car is travelling at 30 mph. The driver sees a rock in the road 20 m away and brakes. Does the car hit the rock?

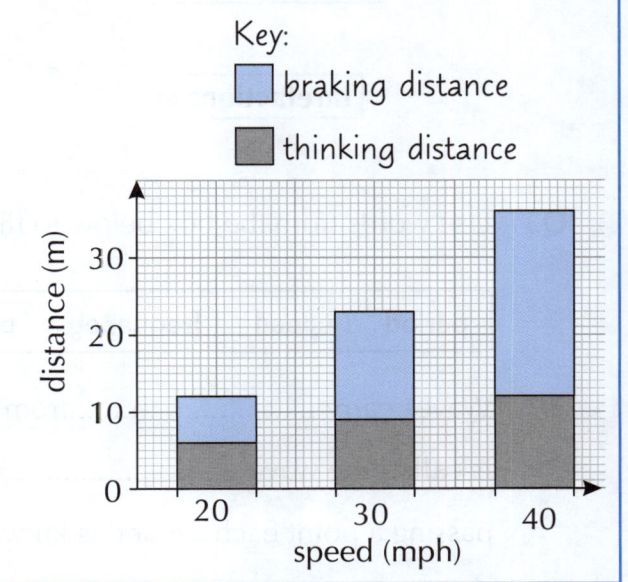

Topic P5 — Forces

Topic P6 — Waves

Waves: The Basics

Let's dive into the wonderful world of waves. For one type of wave, the vibrations go up and down — for the other, the vibrations go back and forth, in the same direction as the wave is travelling.

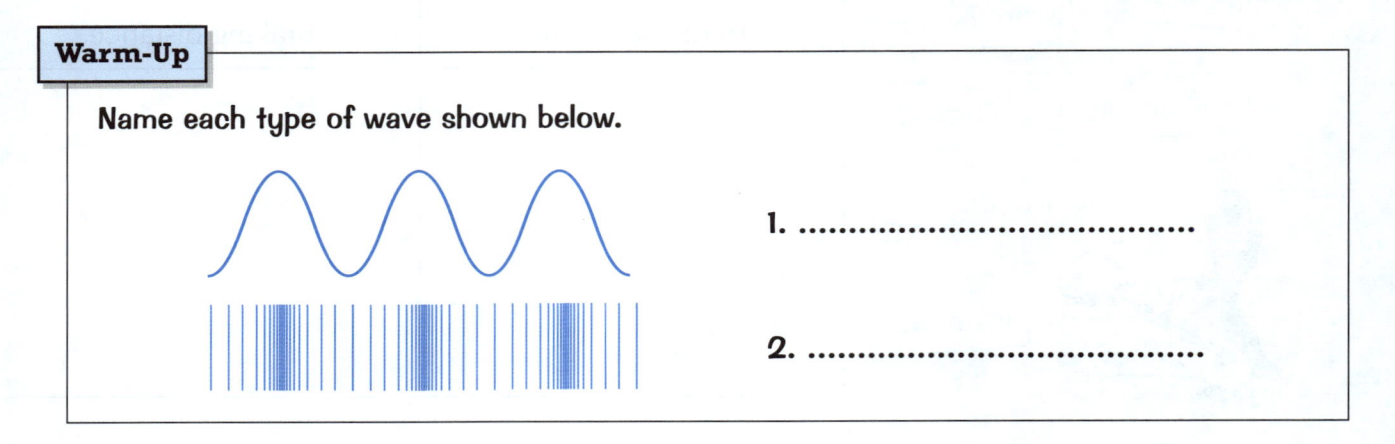

Warm-Up

Name each type of wave shown below.

1. ....

2. ....

Q1 Choose from the words given to complete the labels on the wave below.

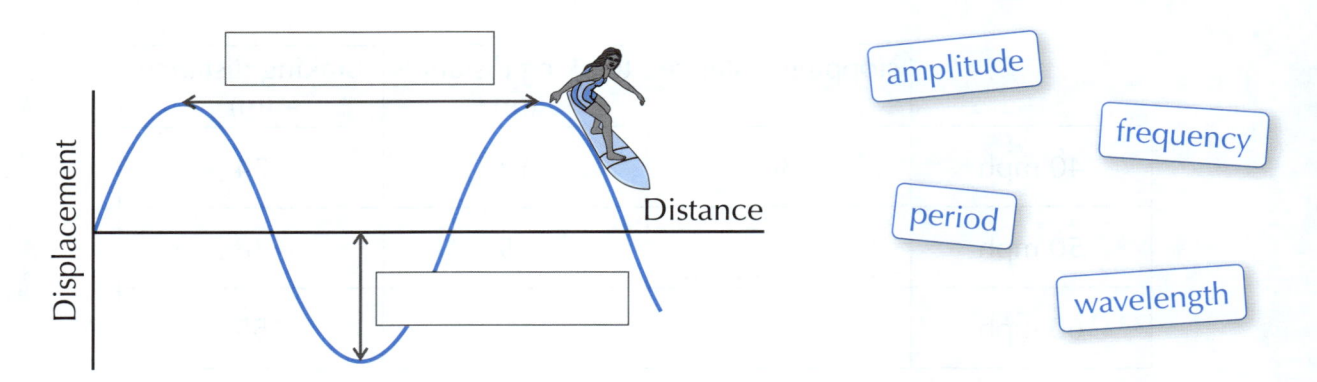

amplitude   *frequency*   *period*   *wavelength*

Q2 Longitudinal waves have compressions and rarefactions. Draw lines to match each word to its description.

compressions — where the particles are spread out

rarefactions — where the particles are squished together

Q3 Use words from the box below to fill in the gaps.

| period | speed | frequency | particles | energy |

Waves carry .... from one place to another. How fast they travel is called the wave .... The number of complete waves passing a point each second is known as the ....

Q4 Which type of wave is each statement about?

	longitudinal	transverse
Vibrations are at right angles to the direction of energy transfer.	☐	☐
Vibrations are in the same direction as the energy transfer.	☐	☐
A sound wave is an example of this type of wave.	☐	☐
A water ripple is an example of this type of wave.	☐	☐

Q5 Use the equation below to calculate the time period of a wave. The frequency of the wave is 20 Hz.

$$\text{period} = \frac{1}{\text{frequency}}$$

Period = ... seconds

What did the sea say to the beach?
Nothing, it just gave a little wave...

NOW TRY THIS

1) Colin is measuring the speed of water waves using a ripple tank. The dipper moves up and down to produce waves.

   He photographs the shadows cast by the ripples and the ruler. The distance between each shadow line is one wavelength.

   a) Colin measures the total distance across 10 gaps between shadow lines. It is 1.2 m. Calculate one wavelength in metres.

   b) The frequency of the waves is 2 Hz. Calculate the wave speed. Use the equation:

   wave speed = frequency × wavelength

   Use the wavelength you calculated in part a)

   c) Colin floats a cork on the water. How does the cork's movement show that it is the wave that travels, not the water?

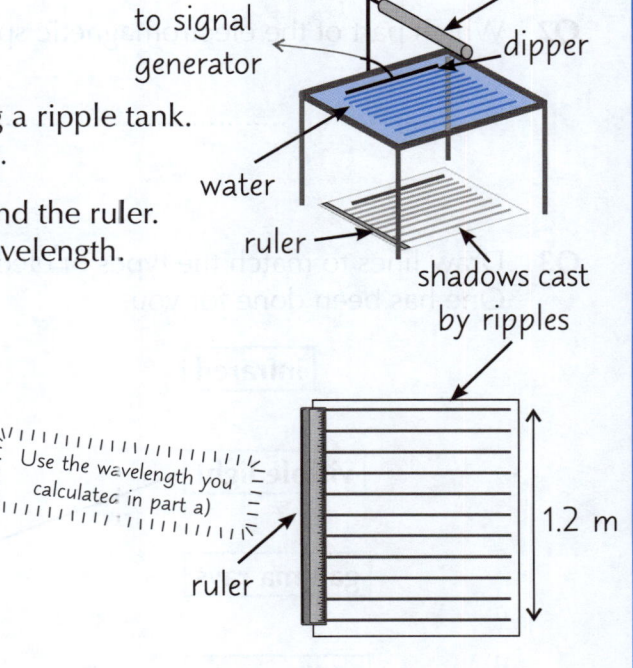

Topic P6 — Waves

Electromagnetic Waves and Their Uses

We use electromagnetic waves for loads of stuff — from TV to cooking to treating cancer.

Warm-Up

Tick either true or false for each statement below.

	True	False
Electromagnetic waves form a continuous spectrum.	☐	☐
Electromagnetic waves move material from one place to another.	☐	☐
Electromagnetic waves are longitudinal waves.	☐	☐
All electromagnetic waves travel at the same speed in a vacuum.	☐	☐

Q1 Put these groups of waves in the right places to complete the electromagnetic spectrum.

Ultraviolet   Gamma rays   Microwaves

| Radio waves | | | Infrared | Visible light | | X-rays | |

Low frequency ⟶ High frequency

Q2 Which part of the electromagnetic spectrum can our eyes detect?

....

Q3 Draw lines to match the types of electromagnetic waves to their uses. One has been done for you.

infrared — sending TV and radio signals

visible light — treating cancer

gamma rays — sending data through fibre optic cables

radio waves — cooking food

Topic P6 — Waves

Q4 Put these types of radiation in order of increasing wavelength.
Use the numbers 1 to 4, where 1 is the shortest wavelength.

☐ ultraviolet   ☐ gamma   ☐ microwaves   ☐ visible light

Q5 Circle words in blue to make these sentences correct.

Electromagnetic waves transfer **matter / energy** from a source to an absorber.

For example, an electric heater emits **infrared radiation / X-ray radiation**.

When objects absorb these electromagnetic waves, energy is

transferred to the object's **thermal / chemical** energy stores.

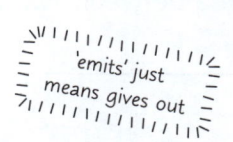

'emits' just means gives out

Q6 Use words from the box below to fill in the gaps.

| infrared | frequency | gamma | atoms | radiation |

Changes in .... produce electromagnetic radiation.

Each different change produces a different .... of electromagnetic wave.

A change in the nucleus of an atom can produce .... radiation.

Wave away all your electromagnetic spectrum troubles...

NOW TRY THIS

The surface of an object affects the amount of electromagnetic radiation it gives out.
This question is about an experiment you can do to investigate this.

Linda sets up the equipment on the right to investigate the
amount of infrared radiation emitted by different surfaces.
Each side of the cube has a different surface.
The cube is filled with boiling water.

1) Linda records the amount of infrared radiation
   emitted from each side of the cube.
   Her results are shown on the bar chart.

   a) Which surface emitted the most infrared radiation?

   b) Which surface emitted the least infrared radiation?

   c) Give one thing that Linda must keep
      the same during the experiment.

   d) State a hazard involved in this experiment.

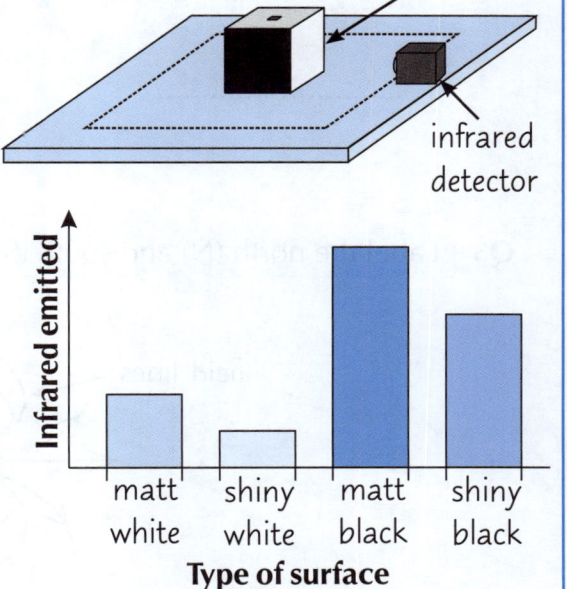

Topic P6 — Waves

Permanent and Induced Magnets

Magnetism is a bit of a tricky subject. Never fear, these questions will guide you through it.

Warm-Up

Circle the words in black to make these sentences correct.

Two magnetic poles that are the same **attract / repel** each other.

Two magnetic poles that are different **attract / repel** each other.

The force between two magnetic poles is a **contact / non-contact** force.

Q1 The diagram shows a bar magnet and some paperclips made of a magnetic material. Circle the paperclip on which the magnetic force is strongest.

Which type of force is acting between the magnet and the paperclips?

☐ an attractive force   ☐ a repulsive force

Q2 Name two magnetic materials.

1. ....   2. ....

Q3 Label the north (N) and south (S) poles on the bar magnet below.

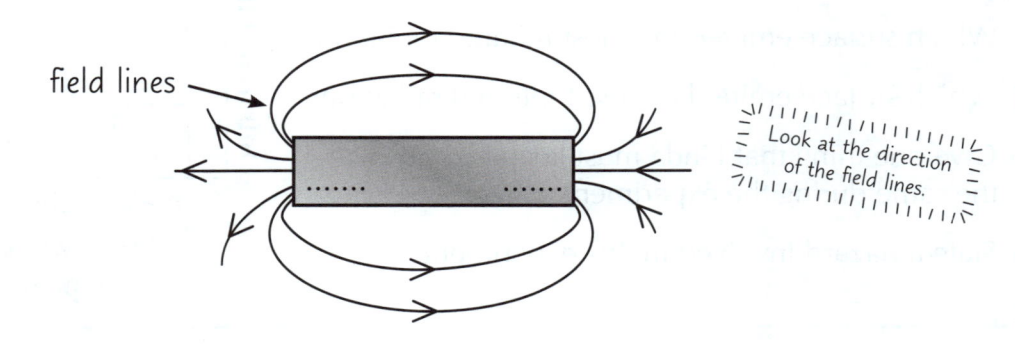

field lines

Look at the direction of the field lines.

A bar magnet and its magnetic field is shown below.
Circle the strongest parts of the magnetic field.

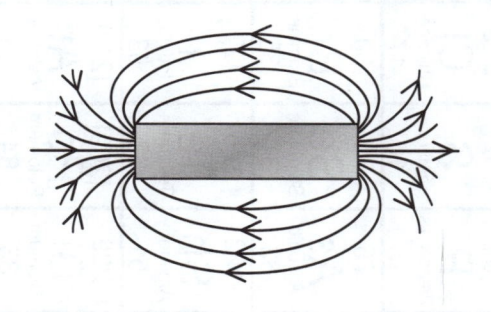

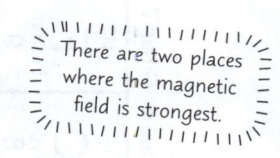

There are two places where the magnetic field is strongest.

Explain how you know that the magnetic field is strongest at these points.

....

....

Q5 Which statements are true? Tick two boxes.

☐ Induced magnets always have a magnetic fields.

☐ Permanent magnets and induced magnets always attract each other.

☐ Permanent magnets lose their magnetism when taken away from induced magnets.

☐ Induced magnets only become magnetic when they are placed in a magnetic field.

NOW TRY THIS

Magnetism is never attractive to me...

Magnetism may be very useful, but that doesn't make it easy.
Here's another question just to test you a little bit further...

1) A compass is placed on an empty desk in a classroom.

   a) In which direction does the compass needle point?

   b) Describe how the student could use the compass to plot the magnetic field pattern of the bar magnet. The student has a piece of paper and a pencil too.

Topic P7 — Magnetism

The Periodic Table

	Group 1	Group 2											Group 3	Group 4	Group 5	Group 6	Group 7	Group 0
Period 1							1 H Hydrogen 1											4 He Helium 2
2	7 Li Lithium 3	9 Be Beryllium 4											11 B Boron 5	12 C Carbon 6	14 N Nitrogen 7	16 O Oxygen 8	19 F Fluorine 9	20 Ne Neon 10
3	23 Na Sodium 11	24 Mg Magnesium 12											27 Al Aluminium 13	28 Si Silicon 14	31 P Phosphorus 15	32 S Sulfur 16	35.5 Cl Chlorine 17	40 Ar Argon 18
4	39 K Potassium 19	40 Ca Calcium 20	45 Sc Scandium 21	48 Ti Titanium 22	51 V Vanadium 23	52 Cr Chromium 24	55 Mn Manganese 25	56 Fe Iron 26	59 Co Cobalt 27	59 Ni Nickel 28	63.5 Cu Copper 29	65 Zn Zinc 30	70 Ga Gallium 31	73 Ge Germanium 32	75 As Arsenic 33	79 Se Selenium 34	80 Br Bromine 35	84 Kr Krypton 36
5	85 Rb Rubidium 37	88 Sr Strontium 38	89 Y Yttrium 39	91 Zr Zirconium 40	93 Nb Niobium 41	96 Mo Molybdenum 42	98 Tc Technetium 43	101 Ru Ruthenium 44	103 Rh Rhodium 45	106 Pd Palladium 46	108 Ag Silver 47	112 Cd Cadmium 48	115 In Indium 49	119 Sn Tin 50	122 Sb Antimony 51	128 Te Tellurium 52	127 I Iodine 53	131 Xe Xenon 54
6	133 Cs Caesium 55	137 Ba Barium 56	139 La Lanthanum 57	178 Hf Hafnium 72	181 Ta Tantalum 73	184 W Tungsten 74	186 Re Rhenium 75	190 Os Osmium 76	192 Ir Iridium 77	195 Pt Platinum 78	197 Au Gold 79	201 Hg Mercury 80	204 Tl Thallium 81	207 Pb Lead 82	209 Bi Bismuth 83	[209] Po Polonium 84	[210] At Astatine 85	[222] Rn
7	[223] Fr Francium 87	[226] Ra Radium 88	[227] Ac Actinium 89	[261] Rf Rutherfordium 104	[262] Db Dubnium 105	[266] Sg Seaborgium 106	[264] Bh Bohrium 107	[277] Hs Hassium 108	[268] Mt Meitnerium 109	[271] Ds Darmstadtium 110	[272] Rg Roentgenium 111	[285] Cn Copernicium 112	[286] Uut Ununtrium 113	[289] Fl Flerovium 114	[289] Uup Ununpentium 115	[293] Lv Livermorium 116	[294] Uus Ununseptium	

Relative atomic mass → 11 B Boron 5 ← Atomic (proton) number

The Lanthanides (atomic numbers 58-71) and the Actinides (atomic numbers 90-103) are not shown in this table.

SAFBW41